BORN AMISH

Life Before the Ex-communication

ANN STOLTZFUS TAYLOR

Year of the Book
135 Glen Avenue
Glen Rock, PA 17327

Print ISBN: 978-1-949150-27-8
Ebook ISBN: 978-1-949150-64-3

Ann Stoltzfus Taylor
brilliance@comcast.net
PO Box 10246
Lancaster, PA 17605
www.DrAnnTaylor.com

Cover photo: Cathy Kornfield
Author photo: Steve Cicero

I have tried to recreate events, locales, and conversations from my memories of them. In order to maintain their anonymity in some instances I have changed the names of individuals and places, I may have changed some identifying characteristics and details such as physical properties, occupations, and places of residence.

Dedication

In memory of Samuel Esh, a long-standing family friend, who helped me understand the mysteries of my Amish childhood.

TABLE OF CONTENTS

Preface

I can still feel the shock of my father and grandfather's excommunication as though it happened yesterday.

My life as a fourteen-year-old Amish girl was about to change drastically that fateful Sunday afternoon in the spring of 1954. It all happened so quickly – at a special meeting after church, in a neighbor's farmhouse.

Lunch was delayed. We kids waited patiently for the meeting to end. Or perhaps not so patiently after the first hour or two. Women were standing around the house, some nursing their babies, others staying with the food they had prepared in the kitchen. A simple affair. My favorite spread of a light syrup mixed with peanut butter, home-made rolls, snitz pie, pickled red beets, home-canned pickles, and a drink.

We girls stayed inside the house. The boys were off in the barn, where the menfolk ordinarily might be seen after a church service. But not this day.

All the men were in a special meeting with the bishop, sitting on backless benches in another room of the farmhouse. They were ardently discussing Ike Smoker's machine shop, a factory that had grown too big and too modern for Bishop Dan (Stoltzfus) to accept. The shop was in violation of several church rules.

Close to a dozen men, like my father and grandfather, were seated on a separate bench to show support for their good friend, Ike. Some sat together as father-son groups.

They wanted the bishop to "get off Ike's back and let him run his business. Change the rules, if necessary." But others were pressuring Bishop Dan – my grandfather's brother – to enforce the existing rules and ex-communicate Ike if he refused to sell his business. New things were happening in that shop. *"What will that lead to,"* they feared. *"It must be stopped."*

By all reports, tempers were hot in that meeting. No one was listening and nothing got resolved until Bishop Dan would make his decision. He was the boss. As an ordained man of God in the Amish Church, he was taking total authority over this new factory issue that no one quite knew how to deal with, or resolve, back then in 1954.

The meeting came to an end when Bishop Dan[1] ex-communicated Ike Smoker and the dozen or so men who supported him. My father and grandfather were in that group.

News of what happened in that special meeting spread like wildfire as the men came to the tables for the noon meal. I don't remember what happened next, except that I was in shock.

Of course, I was excited by the new Buick that showed up in our driveway, and my eyes popped wide open when I saw my sixty-year-old grandfather behind the wheel of a car for the first time in his life. I marveled at the electricity

[1] Bishop Dan was my grandfather's younger brother, who my family knew as Uncle Dan. These two brothers were different. This wasn't their first clash, but no one (in or out of the church) would ever have expected this ex-communication to happen. Grandpa (Abe Stoltzfus) was sixty years old when this occurred and his brother, Dan, was fifty-nine. I'm told they never spoke to each other again.

that brought modern conveniences to our house and barn, but my mood quickly changed when I lost my childhood friends after that school year.

Losing those friendships was one of the hardest things that ever happened to me, but I moved on, and so have the Old-Order Amish in Lancaster County.

I've lived a good life and I'm happy about the flourishing businesses these Amish are now allowed to have, some even bigger than Ike's ever was. But I have a need to know (and talk about) what really happened that Sunday in 1954. That's why I'm writing this book. I'm also curious about the family values of my upbringing and how they might have influenced me and the choices I've made in life.

I previously shared examples of my upbringing in a workbook about our potential brilliance. Now I'm back again – to the childhood mysteries that remind me of the Nancy Drew books and the Hardy Boys series I voraciously read as a child, in bed, under the covers and by the light of a very bright flashlight.

PART I

MY EARLY CHILDHOOD

1 | FAMILY TIES

The doorbell woke our town doctor out of a deep sleep on February 28, 1940, just hours before leap year. My father was standing outside in the cold, desperately hoping Dr. Buri was available for a home delivery. Mom had gone into early labor, not knowing exactly what to expect since I was her first child.

Babies weren't new to Mom. She was one of fifteen children from an Old-Order Amish family in Lancaster County, Pennsylvania. She had helped raise a few of her younger brothers and sisters, but this premature little five-pound baby, was her very own, soon to be named Anna.

"You were so tiny that Dad carried you around on a pillow," Mom once told me. "He was afraid of letting you fall." Six months later, he was carrying me to the farm – where Aunt Anna and Grandma took care of me – while Mom worked at the local knitting mill two days a week, from eight in the morning until closing time.

As months passed, Dad pulled me along to the farm in a little red express wagon covered with blankets and other comforts that made that bumpy ride on the "Pig Lane" more comfortable.[2]

---

[2] The Pig Lane was a short dirt road that connected our house on the Old Philadelphia Pike (PA 340) to the family farm on the corner at

Amish married couples, like my parents, Gid and Lizzie Stoltzfus, were expected to raise their children on a farm, but that hadn't happened yet. We didn't move to Dad's family farm until I was seven. Until then, Dad sold cheese at Booth's Corner Farmer's Market outside Philadelphia. Plus, he helped butcher the chickens that were sold at his father's stand, next to his.

Businesses were allowed by the Amish bishops back then, but they had to stay small. They couldn't be fast-growing like Ike Smoker's.

My parents' first house sat at the edge of the town of Intercourse, close to Zimmerman's Store, where one scene from the movie *Witness* was filmed, starring Harrison Ford.

Some think this town got its name from the intersection of two major roads or from the mile-long horse racetrack, known as "enter-course." Others attribute it to the Cross Keys Tavern, a famous old colonial inn, built at the intersection in 1754.[3]

A community developed around the inn, known as Cross Keys, in 1754. A town was laid out in 1814, with a name change to Intercourse.[4] Amish settled in the area in

---

the Newport Road (PA 772). Today this lane is paved and it has a new name – Hollander Road.

[3] Intercourse Civic Association. (1954). *200th Anniversary.* Intercourse, PA: self-published, p. 63.

[4] Ibid., p. 63.

the early 1800s and the town slowly became a business hub for the surrounding countryside.

Figure 1: Intercourse sign.

Figure 2: Cross Keys Hotel. Site of the first building in Intercourse.

Our four-bedroom frame house was modern for its time, especially for an Amish family. It was more comfortable and efficient than the eighteenth-century Amish farmhouses around us. Those were difficult to heat, and often lacked indoor bathroom facilities.

Dad's parents had financed the building project, right after Mom and Dad were married in December 1938, when his family was feeling the hardship of the Great Depression, which began in 1929 and ended a decade or so later.

Dad's parents, like many Amish farmers, were struggling in those scary times. Bills were piling up at one point and the bank mortgage was three or four months late. They could have lost the farm, according to Uncle Ben, but Aunt Sadie and Grandma saved that from happening. They came up with the idea of selling chickens and homemade bread at Booth's Corner Farmer's Market. Sadie and her husband were already doing well at their own stand, but they needed help in meeting the demand for chickens.

Farmers, like my grandparents, may have been a little better off during the Depression than most since they could sell farm produce – like the garden vegetables they grew – and the chickens they butchered for market. The local banks helped good customers like my grandparents, but there was only so much they could do. Bankers had to "watch their pennies" too, as the expression goes.

Thanks to the busy farmer's market sales, my grandparents' finances turned around quickly, including the mortgage payments which were then easily caught up.

"Who built the house where I was born?" I asked Mom one day. She said it had been built by Dad and his younger brother, Sam. But others helped – like the men from their church district, and the carpenters they had worked for in their teenaged years. Uncle Davy remembers Dad digging out the basement all by himself with a one-horse piece of equipment. This was a big job for a 22-year-old Amish man with no access to electricity or hydraulic equipment.

The lot for the house had been a gift from Dad's grandparents, Sammy and Annie Stoltzfus, or so I was told. They owned the farm behind us, which included a *Daudy haus*,[5] where they would live out their retirement years. The farm would be sold to their youngest son, Stef, and his wife Rebecca.

I admired my energetic little great-grandmother, Annie, who I was named after, and who I knew as "*Grosmommy*." I remember her kind words and the goodies she always had for me – like a big pocket full of candy under her black apron, and colored popcorn she kept in a cupboard known as "the combine."

Drop-ins were always welcome at this *Daudy haus*. No one ever left without a snack or a meal – which included the homeless men (known then as "tramps") who walked the country roads in the summer and camped out on the porch of the one-room schoolhouse in our neighborhood.

---

5 *Daudy haus* is an Amish name for the living quarters next to the farmhouse where elderly parents are watched over by grown children in their retirement years.

Mom was energetic, too. Work and daily chores, done the old-fashioned way, kept her busy... but sewing was her favorite. She assumed her role of making our Amish clothes, yet treated it more like a hobby than a job. She spent a great deal of time in her sewing room next to the kitchen, where my wooden toy box was kept. It had been made by her father.

I played with my toys while Mom sewed. Sometimes, she would turn her chair around to play with me – on the floor or in the playpen. But she was often so deeply engrossed in her projects that I entertained myself, playing with my toys, or watching the treadle (a peddle that rocked back and forth to power the machine) go up and down under the movement of her feet, until I fell asleep in a hypnotic state.

Memories of Grandma's house are different. Although I have inklings of a crib somewhere, I mostly remember being with people. Getting in the way and trying to help. That was fun for me! More fun than playing with toys – all by myself.

Following Mom around was fun, too. I remember standing at our kitchen counter on a step-stool, licking cake batter from Mom's spatula and helping her wash the potatoes she was peeling for dinner. We laughed a lot, just like we did in the bathtub where she would scrub my little body with a washcloth, determined to get the dirt behind my ears and between my toes where it tickled. It was hard for me to stay in one place in that old Victorian tub, so big I kept sliding from one side to the other. But, of course, that was part of the fun, and so was the little rubber boat that bobbed its way around the water's edge, mostly on its side.

Grandma had grown up with a last name of Stoltzfus, but her mother, Nancy, was a Fisher. People said Grandma was a lot like her mother, who I never knew since Nancy passed away three years before I was born. Grandma was quiet, very patient with her children, and somewhat of a homebody. She didn't go to the farmer's market like her daughters, but she helped her daughter Miriam make the homemade bread that was sold at the stand, and she watched over things at home.

Young farm boys like hers ate everything she put on the table, three times a day; and they were mischievous enough to need her supervision. My dad was her eldest, and most of his siblings still lived at home with Grandma. They were a lively group of adventurous kids – fun to be with, always telling stories and joking around.

Years later, Dad's youngest brother, Davy – a handsome guy born in 1936 – joked about not knowing back in those days that there was anything of the chicken besides the neck. He was always seated at the end of the table, next to his father, and as the food got passed around, he was the last served. He would have been just two or three years old when my grandparents started going to market, while Dad was already in his early twenties. Nineteen years made a big difference in their age... and appetites!

Davy spent twenty years in the Marines, then retired as a Captain in 1975, while stationed at Camp Lejeune. He had signed up back when he was a member of the Mennonite Church that didn't believe in going to war. They were pacifists. Other church members came to his parents' house, trying to convince Davy not to go into the service, even though he'd already signed up. But Davy said his parents never judged him for joining the Marines, even though it wasn't their way of life.

"They just always wanted the best for me."

Grandma had a burning desire for things to "go right" for her family and mostly they did. However, there were times she would retreat to a quiet place in the house, maybe to get away from the noise or to deal with the dark mood of her concerns and fears that might have started in her childhood, which wasn't the best.

Her father had been known among the Amish as "Wild Gid," since he was not a "good Amishman" in the way he did things. Apparently, Gid was a spender who didn't manage his money well. So, her family had moved frequently, including a few rented farms and a house at the town intersection in Intercourse. Some say he bet on horses, didn't always pay his bills, drank too much of the strong drink he brewed for himself, made poor decisions, and got involved in a few other things that were not acceptable in the Amish culture.

Grandma and her siblings didn't repeat their father's behavioral patterns. They made much better decisions and did well in life, which included the relationship with their children and grandchildren. They were great people, though not all Amish.

Mom had her heartache, too. I didn't understand the undivided attention to her sewing machine when I was little, just two or three years old. But maybe it helped her deal with the gut-wrenching pain of losing her sixteen-year-old brother, Amos, to a farm accident the day before Christmas in 1941, soon after Mom's third wedding anniversary.

Amos had been standing by the barn when a team of field horses backed up a farm wagon so fast he couldn't get out of the way. His body was badly crushed and he died instantly.

The younger siblings were immediately taken out of school. A message to "come home" was sent to an older brother, Jonathan, who was serving his country as a conscientious objector during World War II. Amish neighbors dropped by to do the daily chores, like making the meals, doing the milking, and helping with the funeral arrangements that would be held in the farmhouse. The family wouldn't be celebrating Christmas the next two days, because of other things that had to be done.

The news about Amos' death spread like wildfire. People stopped in to offer their condolences and to say goodbye to Amos, whose badly mangled body may already have been lying in a plain pine coffin kept in a side room.

This tragedy hit the family hard, including Mom who had helped raise her little brother Amos.

Grandma Lapp – whom I knew as "Mommy" – was in shock at first, and kept telling people she was sorry she hadn't given Amos some of the homemade chocolate candy she put away for Christmas Day. "He always liked that candy so much," Mommy kept saying. If only she could go back and redo that decision. But of course, she couldn't. Her precious son, Amos, had gone to heaven so it was best to let go of her guilt and remorse.

The sadness of his death was enough for Mommy to bear. Amos' body would now be lying in the Buena Vista Amish Cemetery, alongside two other sons who had died as infants.

Grandpa Lapp – "Daudy" – didn't talk about his grief, but I remember his hair turned white. He didn't show his feelings in an open kind of way, but I know he felt the loss deeply. He loved his children and grandchildren "a whole lot," although we didn't always know how much, since neither he nor my father were huggers. Of course, they never used "the L word." You had to see their love in other ways, like the look in their eyes or the special things they did for you.

Family became more important after Amos' death. My mother's parents began to visit us many Saturdays, and we drove to their house one or two Sundays a month. Mom and her mother were always there for each other, but there were no phone calls when things got tough. A postcard sent by U.S. Mail was their main connection between visits, along with chatty letters for which both women were known.

Get-togethers weren't easy for Mom's family back then, in my early childhood. Buggy rides were time-consuming and Amish families, at that time, didn't hire drivers for local trips. What might have been a fifteen- or twenty-minute drive in a car from our home to theirs took over an hour by buggy, starting with the harnessing of the horse. After working so hard to get to our house, Mommy would stay all day to help Mom with a sewing or canning project they both enjoyed.

Daudy, on the other hand, would always leave to do other things, since Dad worked at the farmer's market on Saturdays. However, he must have stayed at our house long enough for me to bond with him. I remember sitting on his lap and playing with his long beard that was turning white, or I would just simply babble. He'd tell me how big I'd grown and make me laugh with "horsey rides" I'd take on one leg at a time, until he needed a break.

Following that short visit, Daudy would move on to the next activity on his Saturday calendar. Sometimes he'd go to a local auction, or drive to Irishtown Road in Ronks to see his sister, Mary, and her husband, John F. Lapp. Or maybe he'd drive to New Holland to visit his brother, John K. Lapp, who was an Amish minister.

Daudy seemed to prefer his sister though, maybe because he was a friend of her husband. But then again, he really liked his sisters, Katie and Susie, too, and often stopped by to see them. Daudy had a brother, Jake, who lived in Buena Vista, but family said Daudy criticized him for being too lenient with his boys – not strict enough. Another Mary in the family argued Jake must have done something right since all his children stayed Amish.

Daudy liked going to the Intercourse Community Sale that was held behind Zimmerman's Store on the first Saturday of every month. He enjoyed the excitement of the auction block and the people he got to see, but he also knew a bargain when he saw one, like a child's rocker he purchased for me.

Mommy, my mother's mother, didn't like all the *gamach* (confusion) of a public sale. She was a homebody who preferred the company of her family, but she didn't try to keep her husband from his interests. She had twelve children who kept her busy.

The Intercourse Community Sale was set up in 1932 by Willis Zimmerman, who owned Zimmerman's Store; and Vic Kling, the town auctioneer. Anyone could bring items to sell. This activity got people through the tough financial times of the Great Depression with used furniture, household items, and farm implements that could be bought or sold. It was also a way to bring in outsiders who would not only spend their money at the sale, but who would also make purchases from the town merchants.

Growth in size and popularity brought attendance, at peak times, to over a thousand, which included the locals like my family, as well as "people from great distances who came to observe the life and customs of the Pennsylvania Dutch Country." [6]

This sale was a fun place to be as I got a little older. Seeing friends and meeting new people was great and so was the melodious chant of the auctioneer. But what I liked best was eating hot dogs and homemade soup, sold at the concession stand. I kept going back for more until it was time to go home... or until I ran out of cash.

---

6 Intercourse Civic Association. (1954). *200th Anniversary.* Intercourse, PA: self-published, pp. 116-117.

Figure 3: Daudy (Sam Lapp) at the Community Sale, mid-1950s. Photo by Melvin Horst.[7]

[7] This photo later appeared on the cover of a book by Elmer Lewis Smith entitled *The Amish People* (New York: Exposition Press, 1958). While handing me a copy of the original photograph in May 1981, the photographer, Melvin Horst, told me this story: "I followed your granddad around that sale for several hours since he was avoiding me. He was surprised when the flash went off in my camera, which was hidden under the side of a farm wagon a good distance away."
I thanked Mel for taking the photograph since it's the only good image my family has of Daudy. Fortunately, we also have one of Mommy, which I took at a family reunion many years ago. "Don't take my picture," Mommy had yelled with a smile on her face, but it was too late. It had already been done. At that very moment I was torn between Mommy's Amish culture that didn't allow picture-taking, and my desperate need for a photo to remember her.

2 | Family Roles

I was a curious little Amish girl from an early age, out to experience life in the best way I knew how. Mom let me be "me," within the context of a group-oriented culture that frowned on individualism. She liked my independence, but I also took on the role of "mother's little helper" at age three, when my first sister Susie Ann came along. Mom quit her job to be a full-time homemaker.

My "mother's helper" role continued as the other kids came along, and I was okay with it because of the bonding that happened. I never wanted to be an only child.

I didn't even have any cousins my age since Dad had been the eldest of his family and Mom was the first to be married in hers. But second cousins like Lissie, the twins (Ada and Anna), and a few others filled the gap. They became my playmates from infancy on up.

They were the children of Dad's fun-loving uncles, whom I knew as John, Stef, Nick and Squirrely. Their sister, Levina, was part of this family too, but I didn't get to know her children since they lived in another district. Another sister, Rebecca, died before I was born and Uncle Dan (the bishop) had no children my age.

Stef was ordained as a minister when I was six,[8] but my family never called him "uncle" the way we did Dad's Uncle Dan. Stef and Dad grew up as friends, the same age, and were married the same year. They even had firstborn baby girls, nineteen days apart. Stef's daughter, Lissie, and I were very good friends, known for our mischievous behavior. But Mom once told Stef not to always blame me for everything, which he was doing. "It's both of them," she said.

One Sunday when church was hosted at our house, Lissie and I got caught painting our lips with red, heart-shaped valentine candy. Stef, the minister, was concerned about this behavior, but Mom saw it as silly girl play, deserving a comment in Pennsylvania Dutch, like, "Schick dich." (Behave yourself.). We never did it again.

My father's family ran a 120-acre dairy farm where we moved when I was seven. But until then we lived a quarter of a mile from the farm – in our first house, where I loved doing things with my parents.

[8] Ministers in the Amish church are chosen by lot. Men who get ten votes from their church district are lined up at a table of books, one for each man. One of the books has a piece of paper inside it, with the idea that God will lead the right man to that paper – and thus the "chosen man of God."

Figure 4: The Stoltzfus family farm in winter.

Working in the garden was fun. Mom and I pulled weeds and planted seeds. Dad prepared the soil with a harrow and a hoe and he built a scarecrow to keep the birds away. Then, we dressed the wooden thing up in an old straw hat and a white bed sheet that blew in the wind. We tied a bundle of tin pie plates and old spoons to its arms that made noises the birds didn't like, and we put a short fence around the lettuce to keep the bunnies away.

The basement of that house was a nice place to be, even though it was a bit dark and eerie, at times. There were no electric lights and the windows were too small to let in much daylight, so Mom and Dad would open the back door for light or use a lantern that hung from the ceiling.

As I got a bit older, Mom would send me down the basement steps, with a flashlight, to bring her something she wanted from the canning shelves. That's where Mom kept the fruits and vegetables she "put up" every summer, and where I could find the pear butter (*ladvark*) that tasted so very good on a cracker or a buttered piece of Mom's homemade bread.

Dad's favorites were the canned peaches and the seven-day pickles, which I didn't appreciate until I got a little older. He also liked eating the raw oysters from a big barrel sitting by the back door of that basement, and so did I. Mom disliked oysters, except in the stew she prepared, but I liked them in whatever way they were served, with a slight preference for "oysters on the half shell." Dad pried those shells open with a shucking knife that stayed on a table by the barrel, but I knew not to touch the knife since it might cut my fingers.

Occasionally I'd see Dad and Grandpa eat those oysters while tasting the grape juice that was fermenting in the wine barrels stacked against a basement wall. Grandpa made this wine for the church communion services held in our district, twice a year. He made it with concord grapes that grew along the fence in our backyard, and he did it as a favor to his younger brother Dan, the bishop.

Our basement was primarily a storage area, but it was also the laundry room for an old-fashioned wringer-style washing machine that was powered by a gasoline engine. On Monday mornings, I'd hear the familiar sound of that Maytag, knowing I'd soon be sliding in the dirty, soapy water when Mom was ready to let it out of a hose, into a drain in the basement floor. There would also be the excitement of grabbing the wet clothes as they came through the wringer and into the laundry basket at my feet.

"Let's go hang out the wash," Mom would say as she grabbed the big, brown wicker basket filled with laundry, ready to be hung out to dry in the sun and the wind. I'd help by handing her the wash pins from a small cloth bag I carried.

This laundry smelled so fresh and nice after hanging on that line for a few hours – unless the farmer behind us decided to spread manure that morning. "*S'macht net gut*" (Doesn't smell good), I'd tell my mother as we took clothes off the line that day, but of course, we had no control over the farmer's schedule. We also had to hope it wouldn't rain because there was no electric dryer as a back-up plan. In that case, the wet laundry would be hung on wooden clothes racks with rungs Mom set up in the kitchen.

A small barn behind our house was home to our carriage horse, Will. It was a storage area for our Amish buggy, the horse feed, and a few garden tools kept in a side room. But this interesting place was off-limits to me unless I was with my parents. They were afraid I'd get too close to Will in his stall, and I was scared of the mice that came in from the fields for the spills by the feed bags. Most scampered away when they heard us coming, but the brave ones stood still and stared me down with their black beady eyes. They gave me "the creeps."

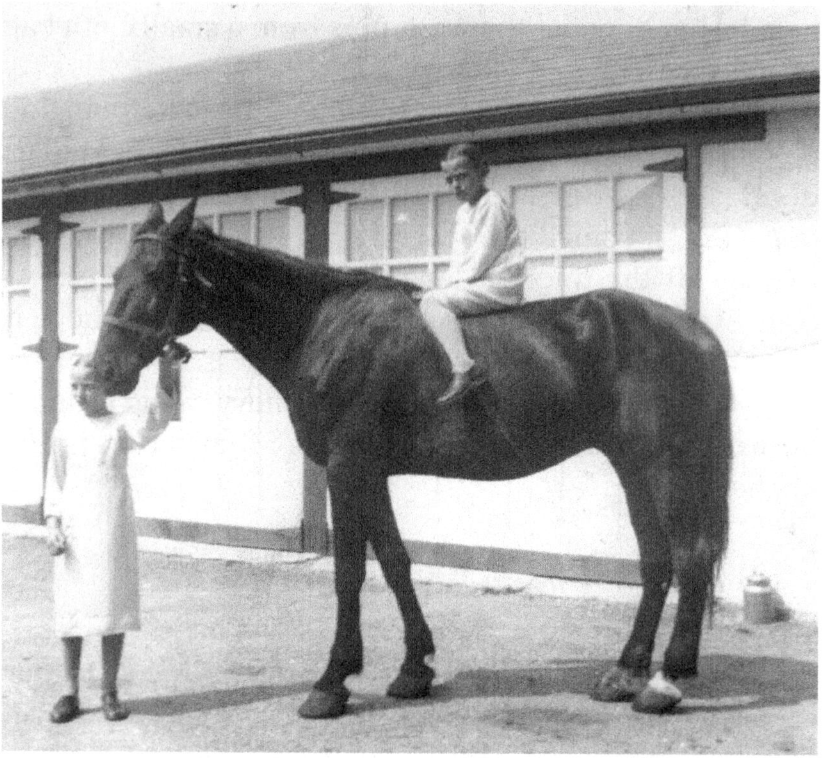

Figure 5: Carriage horse, Will, with sisters Susie Ann (holding the halter) and Priscilla (seated).

"Don't worry about the mice," Dad told me. "They're more scared of you than you are of them. They don't see well. That's why they run along a wall. But rats are different," he explained. "They will attack if they feel cornered. They also bite."

A rat had attacked Dad in his younger years, while he was cleaning out an old chicken house on the family farm. It ran up his pant leg, scaring him so badly that he quickly dropped his oversized suspender pants and ran. Fortunately, the rat didn't bite!

After telling this story to my friend Rebecca, she chuckled and said, "He may not have had anything under those pants either. The boys didn't back then."

Dad worked away from home in my early years before we moved to the farm. So, as I got to be four or five years old, I followed him to jobs and errands, which kept me stepping. This included frequent trips to his parents' farm, and to the town of Intercourse.

This small town was a lively place where we local folks did our banking and bought most of what we needed from town merchants, which included two grocery stores. It was a business hub for the larger farm community and a place where people raised their children in two-story houses. Kids grew up with friendly neighbors and entrepreneurial role models who worked out of their homes or a business next door.

Figure 6: Intercourse east, 1951. Our first house is in the lower right corner.

Monthly charge accounts were common, bills were paid on time, and people knew each other by name and family reputation. "Charge it," we'd tell the sales clerks at the cash register. No credit cards were needed and nothing was signed. Purchases were often hand-delivered to the house.

We were a self-sufficient little town with basic services like a national bank, a U.S. Post Office, a volunteer fire hall, an elementary and secondary school, a restaurant and motel, an insurance agent and auctioneer, a chiropractor, and a church with a bell that rang on Sunday mornings. There was no police department and no crime – only teenaged pranks. We didn't lock our doors.

There was always a town physician as I was growing up. Dr. Buri, who delivered me, sold his family practice to Dr. Bauer when he moved on to Lancaster General Hospital, in their psychiatric unit. Dr. Hartman was the town chiropractor for most of my growing up years, and was assisted by his wife, Carolyn, who also told Bible stories to local kids attending her classes.

Hard-working entrepreneurs ranged from bee keeper, shoe repairman and blacksmith, to plumber, roofer, house painter, and appliance store owner. There was even an Amish artist who had been ex-communicated from the Church because of his connections to art dealers in New York City.

Some of the locals worked for companies in this town, like the flour and feed mills, the knitting mill, two furniture-making shops, a tractor dealership and several Amish manufacturing businesses. John Lapp's Buggy and Carriage Shop made wagons and buggies for the Amish and restored antique carriages for wealthy collectors and museum committees. Eli Stoltzfus' Harness Shop was known for its driving harnesses, among other things like leather saddles and Amish straw hats; and Ike Smoker's Elevator Company was fast-growing.

Figure 7: Lapp's Carriage Shop.

3 | END OF WORLD WAR II

I was five years old in May 1945 when sirens blared from the Intercourse Fire Hall, along with all the neighborhood church and school bells.

"Come with me," my father said as he took my hand. "Let's go see what's going on."

Mom, who was expecting her third child at the time, stayed at home with my two-year-old sister.

Excitement was in the air as we walked into town. Obviously, those blaring sirens and bells symbolized something more important than a fire or twelve o'clock noon. Townspeople were standing in groups, talking about the good news they had heard on the radio, and some of the women were crying into their hankies.

Fifty men from the township had served in World War II and four died in action, but now the rest were coming home.[9] The war had ended! The men returning home may even have included two of my Amish uncles who served their country in alternative ways as conscientious objectors (to military service). Mom's brother Jonathan and Dad's brother Sam had been stationed at the Sidling Hill Camp where they worked on conservation projects in the hills and forests of that part of Pennsylvania.

---

9 Intercourse Centennial book. (1954). 200th Anniversary. Intercourse, PA: self-published, p. 77.

Rationing stamps used to purchase sugar, meat, shoes, gas, and rubber tires ended shortly thereafter. Those necessities would no longer be needed on the battlefield.

"Mamm[10] will be happy to hear about the end of the war," my father blurted out as we walked home that day. "She'll have all the sugar she needs for canning this summer."

The sugar shortage had hit Mom hard. Amish women like her used a great deal of it in the canning, cooking, and baking they did "from start to finish." Sugar substitutes were okay for the duration of the war, but they didn't make the food taste nearly as good as the white cane sugar we were accustomed to, or the brown version we liked in oatmeal.

Canning required a great deal of sugar, and was a big event at Amish homes every summer. Ours was no exception. Piles of vegetables from our garden and many baskets of fruit from Kauffman's Fruit Farm in Bird-in-hand were placed in pint- and quart-sized Mason jars for the fall and winter months and stored on floor-to-ceiling shelves in our basement. The pear butter I really liked sat among hundreds of jars of fruits and vegetables like cherries, peaches, pears, tomatoes, green beans, red beets, chow-chow, pickles, apple sauce, watermelon rind, and grape and strawberry jelly.

Freezing may have been better than canning, since it required less sugar, but we didn't own an electric freezer

---

[10] In the Amish years, I knew my parents as Mamm and Datt, but I use Mom and Dad in this book, which is how I remember them from later years. I knew both sets of grandparents as Mommy and Daudy, but in this book I use Grandma and Grandpa for my father's parents – to avoid confusion.

until the early 1950s when one came to our milk house after a diesel-powered engine or generator was installed in the barn – approved by the bishops because of new State regulations, requiring installation of a milk tank that replaced the widely used milk cans.

Life without sugar and home freezers had definitely been an inconvenience. However, the Amish were probably less affected by the wartime shortages in meat, clothing, shoes, rubber tires, and gasoline than the non-Amish who had never lived the self-sustaining lifestyle of Amish farmers.

My family didn't need rubber tires since we did not own cars, trucks, or tractors and used very little gasoline in other engines. Our meat supply came from the family butcher shop and most of our clothes were made on Mom's sewing machine. We could easily skimp on shoes without much of a problem, since Mose Beiler would re-heel, re-sole, and mend our current shoes until they were totally worn out, or "shot." Shoes also weren't a high priority during the summer months when Amish kids went barefooted as soon as it was allowed.

"Wait until you see the first bumblebee," Mom would tell us when we asked for permission to shed our shoes. Her parents gave us the same advice. Not until the autumn though, did the shoes go back on our feet, after Mom and Dad took us shopping for a new pair that was badly needed.

Around this same time, I remember trips to Uncle John and Aunt Lena's house, and watching "dentist" movies played on reel-to-reel and viewed from a white screen set on a pedestal. There would always be a funny man in the film whose decayed tooth got tied to the tail of a dog that ran over things, including the dog house. We laughed at this scene until our bellies hurt and begged to watch it again and again. There were also home movies of the family, including we Amish kids who got a kick out of seeing ourselves on screen.

Uncle John and Aunt Lena did not have children of their own until they adopted Linford in the early 1950s, but they did have a telephone, a TV when it first came out, and Uncle John owned a car with a rumble seat in the back, where my sisters and I liked to sit for rides around town.

Uncle John – J.B. Lapp – was a well-known and well-regarded welder of farm equipment at the border of Chester and Lancaster County. He also sold used farm equipment. He and Aunt Lena would make things fun. Aunt Lena helped Mom wallpaper our bedroom walls a number of times over the years. I think she wanted to teach us how to hang wallpaper ourselves, but we never really learned.

On New Year's Day we'd go to their house for pork and sauerkraut and watch the Mummer's Day Parade on television, beginning around 1949.

4 | The Farm in Buena Vista

Mom had grown up on a 98-acre dairy farm in Buena Vista, Pennsylvania, with dreams of getting married and raising her own children on such a farm. Her parents, Sam and Susanna (Lantz) Lapp, had moved to this place in 1911, a year after they were married.

Figure 8: The farm at Buena Vista. Photo by Cathy Kornfield.

They paid off the farm loan to Daudy's parents in 1919, soon after World War I, and never moved.[11]

This family farm sat close to a Welsh Mountain range at the far southeastern end of Lancaster County, with a mailing address of Gap, Pennsylvania. It's a mile or so from the Chester County line and about a half-mile from the crossroad at Mt. Vernon and Buena Vista Road. No one seems to know how the area got its Spanish name,

[11] The Historical Society of Salisbury Township. (2004). *Buena Vista Revisited.* Gap, PA: self-published, p. 21.

except that it perfectly describes the "beautiful view" of the pristine valley that has not been touched by modern-day developers since Mom's great-grandparents, Joshua and Mary Lapp, settled there in the 1870s after moving from the Stumptown area of Lancaster County.[12]

I have fond memories of Buena Vista, which include the hour-long buggy rides from our house. On nice days, this ride was lots of fun. My little brother would sit up front, between my parents, while my sisters and I were in the back, waving to people in the cars behind us, sometimes wishing we could be driving at their speed, instead of the five miles per hour our horse, Will, lumbered up the road.

Figure 9: Amish horse and buggy. Photo by Cathy Kornfield.

"How much longer?" we'd yell as we passed the rolling hills and the familiar landmarks, close to their farm. Always counting the goats, cows, and horses in the

[12] Lapp, John K. (1986). *Remarks of By-gone Days*. Gordonville, PA: Gordonville Print Shop, p. 4.

meadows, we sang our favorite songs with Mom's help and played games with the silly little magnetic dogs that stuck together in ways that made us laugh.

Our fingers and toes could go numb in that buggy when the temperature dropped below freezing in the cold winter months. But we were protected by gloves and blankets, and the hot irons Mom wrapped in towels to keep our feet warm. All this was nice, but there was very little wiggle room in the back seat for three little girls packed in like sardines in a can. Snacks would have been great, but Mom didn't want to clean up the crumbs in the "hard-to-get-to places" – made even harder because vacuum cleaners were not allowed by our church rules.

Finally, after what seemed like forever, we'd get to the crossroads in Buena Vista. Then, all of a sudden, the horse turned left onto the long farm lane to Mommy and Daudy's house. They were always glad to see us, but they weren't huggers. We'd get a handshake, a smile, and a greeting that felt like a hug. I knew they loved me!

These trips to Buena Vista in our buggy mostly occurred on Sundays from September through May as we kids were growing up, but this changed to a weekday in the summer. Mom would often put us kids into the buggy for the drive to her parents' farm, where she and her sisters helped Mommy with work. I mostly played with the cousins or helped in the garden, but what I liked best was eating potato chips as they were taken out of the hot lard in a big copper kettle. Making pear butter in that kettle was another favorite, because of how much I liked it.

We cousins always found fun things to do on this big farm, or we'd be entertained by Mom's youngest brothers, Mel and Christ, who were nine and ten years older than me. Rides up and down the hilly farm lane in the portable grain bin were my favorites, since the boys made sure those wiggly, wobbly wheels were turning fast enough to make us scream like kids in an amusement park.

"Again, again," we shouted in Pennsylvania Dutch words like "*wittar*" and "*mae.*" Our bellies were sore from laughing but high levels of adrenaline kept us going from one ride to the next until the boys had to go back to work.

Playing in the Pequea Creek at the bottom of the meadow was another favorite. It was a watering hole for the cows and horses, and a place for the cousins to cool off on hot summer days. So, we put our bare feet into the cold water, at the shallow end, carefully stepping over the slippery rocks, trying not to disturb the cows and horses that were coming up for a drink. Or we'd try to catch the little fish, called *minnows,* which was difficult to do without a net.

There were dangers in that creek back then, and we kids were not allowed to go in too deep, where the swift currents might take us downstream, or the big old-fashioned water wheel might suck us in.

Historically, that creek had been known for its raging currents and flash flooding, and I've seen it fill meadows and wash small bridges away. My parents experienced this flooding one dark rainy night while Dad was taking Mom home from a date in an open courting buggy. When they got to the small bridge in Buena Vista, close to my grandparents' farm, the horse stopped, refusing to move ahead. When Dad got out of the buggy to lead him across the bridge, he saw it had washed away.

The horse had saved their lives.[13]

Mommy was a kind woman with a soft voice. She could be insistent or pushy at times, to a point where I'd give in just to satisfy her, but regardless of who she really was, I admired her and paid attention to what she said.

I soon learned that Mommy's answers to my questions were easy to understand. Like the time I asked her why we Amish girls have to wear a white covering (or *kopp*) on our heads. "It's just the way we've always done things," she answered in a matter-of-fact way that made sense to me. As a little girl, I never did understand the more complicated explanation I got from other people.

Mommy loved her garden and the gorgeous view of the valley from her front porch. She enjoyed the canning, cooking, and sewing she did with her four daughters, who followed in her footsteps as a farmer's wife and mother.

Daudy enjoyed the horses on the farm, which included his carriage horse and the handsome Belgians he and the boys trained for the fields. Apples were always available as treats, and a daily pinch of chewing tobacco kept the worms out of their intestines. Feeding schedules were regular and the field horses had rest periods in the

[13] The Pequea Creek still floods sometimes because of run-off from the fields during a heavy rain, but it's much calmer these days. "Farmers don't plow as much as they used to, or as deep," Samuel Esh explained. "They now know this is better for the run-off [from the fields]. The ground on the fields is tighter now, or not as loose, so there is less run-off into the Pequea Creek when it rains, and less flooding into the meadows."

middle of the day, but most of all there was a relationship between man and beast. They were buddies.

Traveling was Daudy's passion. He did a lot of it in the Amish Way of staying with people rather than at motels (although he did that, too). Some think he bought his first field horses from Henry Miller in Goshen, Indiana, who was a good friend over the years, and a minister in his Amish Church District. He and Daudy were traveling buddies, along with a few other Amish men, who traveled by train or hired drivers – never by plane, since that was against church rules.

Mommy did not travel much, because she didn't want to leave her children, or the farm, for more than a day or so. Like my mother, she was family-oriented, while the husbands needed to feel connected to a larger world of people – and places to see.

I traveled to Goshen with my parents when I was seven. Mom's brother Leroy was getting married to Lucy Miller, who he knew because of Daudy's friendship with her brother, Henry.

"They're different than us," I kept telling my mother. Their Amish clothes were a bit fancier than ours, or so I thought. And the accent of the little girl seated on the bench in front of me during the ceremony was different too. More musical – and a lot like the yodeling I was hearing.

"Mamma, *gr'atz mai bouckle"* (scratch my back), the little girl kept telling her mother in that lovely accent I wanted to learn. So, on the long drive home, I kept repeating her words until the accent stuck in my brain, like a broken record.

5 | "NICE THINGS"

My family lived simply, without the modern convenience of electricity, telephones, cars, TVs, or radios, but we liked nice things.

I liked the soft fabrics of the little dresses Mom made for me, her pretty dishes crafted in Germany, Austria, and France, and the colorful flowers she grew inside and out. Her favorites became mine – the African violets, gardenias, geraniums, peonies, gladiolas, lilacs, irises, bleeding hearts, and the pretty annuals that bloomed all summer. Dad loved trees and roses.

Our house was furnished with country-style cupboards, tables, chairs, and other furniture made by the J.S. Ebersol Chair Shop in 1938-39, when the business was first established. This shop was known for its excellent craftsmanship and the hand-painted flowers on the chairs. Collectors bought a lot of it, and the Amish liked the flowers painted on the tables and chairs – made for adults and children.

Figure 10: Ebersol Chair Shop sign.

This Ebersol collection was part of a wedding gift from my mother's parents who gave her most everything she needed to set up housekeeping. This included a few unusual things by modern standards, like a treadle-operated Singer sewing machine, a Maytag wringer washing machine – like those still used by Amish women today – and an ice chest for the kitchen that required delivery of ice blocks several times a week.

Mom's parents could afford to give their first-married daughter this generous dowry, since they were doing well. Their farm had been paid off in 1919. Cash crops and the dairy were profitable, and Daudy made good money from the peddling he did on Fridays in the City of Coatesville.

"People in Coatesville have money," Daudy once told me. Many worked for Lukens Steel Mill that paid good wages, as top producers of steel plates. But good food was difficult for housewives to obtain during World War II when it was needed on the battlefield. So, the women in Coatesville were happy to see Daudy's spring wagon come to their door – with garden produce in the summer and freshly butchered pork and homemade butter in the winter.

Looking at "nice things" kept me occupied at Hager's Department Store in Downtown Lancaster while Dad was measured up for a custom-made *mutza* (Amish jacket), vest, and pants.

Dad wore Mom's home-sewn pants, shirts, and jackets to work every day, but a custom-made suit was nice for church on Sundays and other special occasions, like weddings and funerals. One good suit, a store-bought white shirt, and a pair of shoes that fit well was all he needed for those dress-up occasions, and they could be bought at Hager's.

Shoes that fit were important to Dad since those he had worn as a child had hurt his feet. Then one day a clerk discovered his shoes were much too narrow for his extra-wide size. Because of that experience he preferred to buy shoes for the family from professional clerks who took measurements, like those at Hager's in Lancaster, and later, at Rubinson's Department Store (after they came to New Holland). But as time went on, Dad, bought shoes from Amish men who sold them from catalogs or a small shop by their house. They also took measurements.

The expertise of Haas, the hatter in Downtown Lancaster, was appreciated by Dad too, since his black felt Amish hats were better and softer than those sold at our local stores. Haas also had a great talent for using the hot irons to turn up the brim of Dad's hat, exactly the way he wanted it. Hass knew the church rules about the brim of those hats and sold them according to specifications, but he also knew how to satisfy the whims of his customers.

This was a good thing for my Dad... but I couldn't wait to get out of that shop because it smelled ten times worse than a newly-scorched ironing board cover.

Some of the young Amish boys liked watching the TV that was always on in Haas' shop, but I preferred the downtown stores and shops with all the lovely children's dresses and coats in the windows. I couldn't wear those pretty clothes as a little Amish girl, but Mom would buy me coloring books and doll cut-out books I liked, along with nice soft fabrics for my Amish dresses she made for me. There were certain colors I couldn't have, like red, pink, light blue or bright green, but I didn't much care about that when I was little. My Amish friends didn't wear those colors either.

Downtown Lancaster was an exciting place to be. Except for the time I lost my mother.

City sirens were blaring that day, the trolleys were making their usual clanging noises as they came to the tracks at the square, and drivers were blowing horns at anything that got in their way.

A kind policeman found me standing on the sidewalk, four or five years old, totally bewildered. He was a stranger who couldn't tell me where to find my mother. This was different from our neighborhood at home, where everyone knew my name and where I belonged.

Finally, I was relieved to see Mom walk out the front door of Woolworth's 5 & 10 Cent Store, where she normally bought hairpins, two-edged black combs, straight pins, and other things used by Amish women. Rumors were out that F. W. Woolworth had opened a store in Lancaster City, hoping to attract Amish shoppers who paid with cash.

"It's time to go home," Mom said as we walked away from the policeman to meet Dad at the bus stop in front of the Swan Hotel. We would take the last White Horse Bus out of the city, but there was still enough time to pick up three big bags of hot popped corn from a friendly Greek immigrant who worked out of a narrow building in the "no-hundred" block of West King Street. His popped corn was the best I've ever had and it smelled good, too.

The corn we popped at our house wasn't as tasty even though we used a very good grade of popcorn that Aunt Lucy bought from Amish farmers in Goshen, Indiana. Maybe the corn in the city was popped with the black olive oil from Greece that's the best of its kind – according to my Greek friend, Susie.

6 | Out and About

Seeing the city as a child opened my eyes to a big wide world out there! Home was nice, especially after my two little sisters came along, but I wanted to be out and about.

Dad was my ticket to the outside world, so at age five and six I followed him around like a little puppy dog waiting for its next walk. The two of us would often amble to the family farm, my three steps to his one. Or we'd head up town to the bank, the general stores, or other local businesses.

We'd drive places in the buggy too, which included trips to the local blacksmith, or to the Noah Leaman farm where Dad worked part-time and I played with their twelve-year-old daughter, Pauline. She read children's books to me, taught me how to draw, let me play the piano, rode me around on the back of her bicycle, and she'd dress me up for tea parties on the front porch. Sometimes, I helped Dad feed the horses and mules that Mr. Leaman kept in the big old Victorian barn on the corner of Westview Drive and the Old Philadelphia Pike.

Those local adventures were fun, but my favorites were the Fridays I spent at the Booth's Corner Farmer's Market (near Philadelphia) – where Dad and his family sold chickens, homemade bread, Swiss cheese made in our neighborhood, and whatever else they could muster up, like potatoes from the fields or vegetables from the garden.

On Friday mornings at nine, a group of us would take the hour or so drive to Booth's Corner, which included me, and sometimes Susie Ann. We'd hop into Aaron Stoltzfus' old remodeled taxi cab, and didn't get back home until nine or ten that evening. Everyone would return to the market on Saturday mornings, except Susie Ann and me. Mom didn't want us to be tired for Sundays, or to miss Mommy and Daudy Lapp's Saturday visits to our house.

Dad's sister, Miriam, and his brother, Aaron, rode to market in a truck that delivered most of the produce to the stand and it would be unpacked by the time our group arrived. The trunk of our taxicab was also loaded down with things, including clean blankets for my bed under the counter. But I always kept a small security blanket in the car with me, just in case I got cold, or for the ride home when Grandpa and Aaron were "fussing."

Those two men were friends and distant cousins who enjoyed each other's company, but they were known for teasing, and sometimes they got loud. This mostly happened when Aaron talked incessantly on the late drive home from market, maybe to stay awake, but Grandpa was too tired to listen to a "flapping tongue that wasn't connected to a brain." He wanted to sleep in the back, after working since four or five that morning.

Sometimes Grandpa shut out Aaron's fussing by rolling up the window between the front and back seat of that refurbished taxicab. This would drive Aaron crazy, and he would threaten to remove the window, but this never happened. Either choice was okay with me as long as I got to sit next to an outside window in the back seat, just in case I'd get car sick.

"*Stup*," I'd shriek in Pennsylvania Dutch when the *upchuck* feeling came over me. Everyone in that car knew what I meant, and they also knew the consequences of a delayed response.

Grandpa had a talkative nature that "got on Grandma's nerves" sometimes, even though she loved him "a whole lot." She once suggested that I get married to someone quieter – which I understood from her own need for quiet – but there were lots of things I really liked about Grandpa. He had a great sense of humor and a passion for life I admired. He enjoyed good food, fun company, and stories that made him laugh, and he helped his children in whatever way he could. He was a hard worker, too. Always busy doing something.

Winning at games was important to Grandpa, whether he was playing checkers or corner ball, or going after a real-life goal. He had a competitive nature, especially with his brother Dan. Their checker games were long and drawn out – often lasting for days. Arguments never really got resolved, because they were different in their thinking, and in most every other way.

People wondered if Bishop Dan had a grudge against his brother, or "was he jealous?" Grandpa had a large family while Dan didn't, and among Amish families this was a point of pride.

Uncle Dan always seemed to be going after Grandpa's unmarried sons, scorning their behavior. Playing cards, seen driving a car, or with the brim of the hats not quite right... Grandpa didn't like that either, but he would argue with his brother. "You don't understand boys because you don't have sons of your own," he would tell him.

Uncle Dan had a great deal of authority as an Amish man ordained by God, but Daudy would have liked a little more understanding about the difficulty of raising eight lively boys (compared to his brother's two well-behaved daughters). It also seemed like Dan didn't try to have a relationship with the boys either – always just watching them like a hawk about to pounce on its prey.

Grandpa and Grandma were strict, though. Radios would disappear if they were found and Grandpa wouldn't let his sons or their friends park a car on the farm (while they were Amish). Grandma burned my father's driver's license before he was married.

That license was against the church rules, but she had also heard that her eldest son was planning to go west with three of his friends in the fall of 1938. She was determined to "nip that idea in the bud." Not only because of the license, but because he might lose his girl, Lizzie Lapp, if he waited for the next Amish wedding season in the fall of 1939. Grandma liked my mother.

Figure 11: Planning to go west. My father, 2nd from left.

Grandpa's competitive nature showed up in some of his sons and his oldest daughter, Sadie, who I admired as a sharp business woman. I'd see her paying for things with cash from a long pocket under her apron, which looked like Mommy's and Grosmommy's, but they only kept candy in theirs.

Aunt Sadie and her husband, Amos, did well with the stands they operated at Booth's Corner Farmer's Market. They paid a lot of the bills for a family of nine children, but Amos was passionate about the retired pacers and trotters from the racetrack, which he trained for the Amish carriages. Some thought Amos' horses were overpriced, but an Amish neighbor of his disagreed. "Amos knew horses," Samuel Esh told me, "and I never bought one from him I didn't like. They were worth the price I paid."

Often, I'd see Amos in a training cart on the Old Philadelphia Pike, between their property on the Hatville Road and Zimmerman's Store in the center of town. This straight stretch of road was great for training horses back then when traffic was not as heavy as it is today.

"Hi," Amos would yell, with a wave of the hand that told you a lot about this friendly man who could sell most anything, including the horse he was driving.

Or one might see him racing his horses with a neighbor, Jake Esh, who was just as competitive, if not more so. "Giddyup," they'd yell, with a tap of the reins, as the two horses ran up that straight stretch of road that had once been a community raceway for carriage horses, known as "enter-course."

7 | Elementary School Years

Learning was fun for me, even in the elementary grades, but my first day of school didn't go all that well.

Figure 12: The author in second grade.

"We have a *hutch*," I told Mrs. Carter in an animated tone of voice, but she didn't know my Pennsylvania Dutch word for "colt," so she asked Katie Stoltzfus, one of my older second cousins, to come up to her desk to interpret.

The embarrassment of that incident, coupled with my interest in learning, quickly motivated me to master the English language. I knew just enough to speak to my friends at the Booth's Corner Farmer's Market, but that wasn't good enough for this teacher. She expected more from me, which was great since it stretched my capabilities.

Mrs. Carter was a strict teacher who taught the first four grades in the one-room public schoolhouse on the west end of town. She kept us busy with assignments and classes, but it wasn't all work and no play. We sang along with a piano she played every morning and sometimes after lunch, and there was always a fifteen-minute recess period in the morning and afternoon. Lunch was an hour-long break, which was plenty of time to ride the see-saws, play *kalyover,* and eat the sandwiches, apples, and peanut butter crackers from our tin lunch buckets. Sometimes Mom would surprise me with a Hershey's chocolate bar with almonds, which was my favorite.

That one-room schoolhouse was heated by a big, cast-iron coal stove that also toasted our cheese and bologna sandwiches to perfection. It was tended and stoked twice a day by a local woman we affectionately knew as "Fanny Flapper." She walked so fast and with such zeal that her long skirts flapped from side to side and her arms swung back and forth. She was on a mission!

Most of Mrs. Carter's students remember her as a good teacher and so do I. She was a motivator, and well-organized, but I disagreed with the dunce hat and "the paddling" she used as punishment for breaking her rules. Those infractions could be as minor as forgetting to clear off the top of our desk before running out to recess, coming to class late, sneaking notes to other students, or talking while school was in session. She didn't miss much either, so we thought she must have eyes in the back of her head. I wore that dunce hat a lot – with a sense of humor and in ways that made the other kids laugh, but I managed to stay away from the paddle.

I wasn't a bad kid although I couldn't sit still for two or three hours at a time. I'd get "antsy" and had to move around. I was also a curious student with a voracious need to learn, but it was difficult for me to do all the memorizing Mrs. Carter required. I wasn't good at reciting poems, but I could tell you what I had read in a book and I liked writing stories from pictures on the covers of *Look* magazines she brought from home.

Perfect attendance for the school year was important to me too, since Mrs. Carter gave a book to students who hit the mark. I got one of those perks every year except fourth grade when I missed a day of school to attend Aunt Lydia's wedding. I wanted to wait and go to the wedding after school that day but Mommy Lapp had insisted I be there for the full day-long event... and in exchange, she promised to give me a copy of my favorite book, *Heidi.*

I'm trying to tell you that I wasn't a "straight A" student in those early years, nor was I a teacher's pet. I made A's in the subjects and projects I was drawn to, but I also got B's and C's. I was passionate about learning, but I did it best by reading library books and working on writing assignments.

I wasn't perfect and neither was Mrs. Carter, but I learned a lot and thought learning was fun. She probably wouldn't like what has happened to my penmanship since then, but I can still recite *the alphabet,* the *Pledge of Allegiance,* and *the Lord's Prayer*, which are deeply embedded in my brain, along with the *times table* that has since been made superfluous by calculators.

Mrs. Carter put the idea of college into my head even though that hadn't been her intention. I will always remember the day she pointed to the Amish girls in my third-grade class and told us we would quit school after the eighth grade.

"The rest of you might go to college since it's not against your religion," she told the non-Amish students, who we knew as the *Englisch* or *Englisha*. She didn't explain what "college" was and I certainly didn't know anything about it back then, but the event stuck in my mind.

PART II

THE FARM YEARS

8 | Moving to the Farm

Dad said we'd move to the farm as soon as I could whistle, and it happened just as he said. A horse-drawn farm wagon pulled up to our door early one morning on a warm, breezy day in the spring of 1947, shortly after my seventh birthday. School would soon be over.

This was a happy occasion for Mom who really wanted to be a farmer's wife where she could work alongside her husband and children. Dad wanted the respect of being a good farmer, and I couldn't wait to move to the big playground. My four-year-old sister, Susie Ann, walked around in a daze that day, not always knowing what to do, while two-year-old Priscilla cried hysterically when her big white iron crib was carried to the moving wagon.

Figure 13: The author (age 7) and sister, Priscilla (age 2), in church clothes – at the first family house.

"Make her stop crying," my mother pleaded as she placed Priscilla's little hand in mine.

But Priscilla wouldn't stop – no matter what I said or did. So, I stepped off to the side for a few minutes, trying to get my mind off this frustrating situation.

I moved a few things around on the front porch, waved at cars that went by, and slowly counted to twenty, but nothing changed. Suddenly, the crying stopped. As if by magic. I had simply done what I could, and ignored the behavior I couldn't control.

The last wagonload pulled out of our driveway in the middle of the afternoon, and our family carriage left a little later. We were entering a totally different era of our lives. The house we were leaving would now become home to Dad's parents and three or four grown children. The others had moved on to marriage, or single life away from home.

Grandma was forty-nine years old. Grandpa was fifty-three and my parents were thirty. I was in the first grade. My two sisters were not yet in school, and my only brother, John, would soon be born.

"It's a boy!" Dad announced on June 2nd, after spending time in my parents' bedroom with Mom and Dr. Burie who delivered him. "Yay!" I shouted out – after having waited all those years for a little brother. But John would always be seven years younger than me, with very different childhood experiences.

Mom sang a lot after that, especially in the morning while preparing breakfast. Dad was uptight sometimes – overwhelmed by the responsibilities of running a 120-acre dairy farm. He and a younger brother, Dan, were stretched to the limits of their capabilities, even though they had hired extra help to plant the crops, bring in the hay, fill the silo, and whatever else was needed.

Both men were unbelievably hard workers and well-trained farmers. But there was only so much they could do in a day, especially with mules and old-fashioned farm implements. Tractors would have made things easier, but they wouldn't have had the personality of the mules, and besides, they were against our church rules.

Dad's youngest sister, Syll, helped Mom with her work after we moved to the farm. She was lots of fun! And a big help to Mom while we kids were little and needed time to play. There were geese to chase, dogs and bunnies to hold and cuddle, water from the spring in the meadow to cool our bare feet on a hot summer day, and snowmen and tunnels to build when the drifts were piled high. Toys were slowly added to our collection, like jump ropes, chalk for hopscotch, roller skates, ice skates, scooters, all kinds of balls and a cupboard full of games like Snap, Old Maid, Parcheesi, Chinese Checkers and Monopoly®. The badminton net, croquet set, ping-pong table and baseball diamond which came later, attracted other kids to our farm in a big way.

Figure 14: Siblings John, Priscilla, Susie Ann, and the author.

Cousins were dropped off for the day or an overnight stay, and relatives and friends visited on weekends with their kids.

Figure 15: Susie Ann, John, and Priscilla with the bunnies.

Children from the Bronx – sponsored by the New York Fresh Air Fund – came for two weeks in the summer and often longer. One such child, Eva, was five years old when she started coming to our farm, and she stayed the longest. We all loved Eva a whole lot, but eventually, after graduating from our local high school, she moved on to raise her own family. By then, she could have married a farmer because of all the skills she had so eagerly learned from my parents.

In fact, she was better at those roles than me, who had been born into the culture. I helped my Mom as much as I could, by the time I was ten, but my mind and my interests were often elsewhere.

"I have to go upstairs and read now," I would tell Mom, who seemed to understand.

"Don't be long," she'd tell me when there was work to be done. Dad thought all that reading was "being lazy," but Mom would tell him to let me go (*less sie gay*). "She's done her work."

I missed the people at the farmer's market after we moved to the farm and Dad left the stand. Those stand holders had always made sure I had things to do and plenty to eat, and customers had complimented me for cutting a piece of cheese right to the pound. "How do you do that?" they would ask, knowing I was only six years old and could barely reach the cutting board and the scales, sitting on the table next to the glass case where the cheese was kept.

The owner of the spinning wheel was always happy to see me come to his stand with a handful of dimes from

Dad, given for "something to do." This stand owner knew I was trying to win yet another one of his figurines for my collection that was growing quite nicely, and he knew that my favorites were the painted roosters and clowns he kept on a high shelf.

"Where do you get all those dimes?" he once teased. "Do they grow on trees?"

His idea sounded good to me so I planted several dimes in the crusty patches of soil behind our barn, hoping to see them grow, which of course, never happened. I had a lot to learn about growing things back then, but that wasn't really my interest.

I was crazy about baseball and *kalyov*er and played whenever I had a chance, but I also read lots of library books that calmed me down when things got hectic.

"You check out more library books than most of the others," the librarian once told me.

I always took out the maximum number allowed from the bookmobile she drove around to the schools in our county.

Figure 16: The county library bookmobile, parked outside the schoolhouse in Hatville.

I preferred books to the baby dolls my sisters played with, even though Annabelle was my buddy from the day Uncle Johnny delivered her to our farm.

"You need a doll and here's one for you," he announced with a pleased look on his face. "Her name is Annabelle and she's almost as tall as you."

Aunt Syll liked Annabelle too, since there wasn't much difference in our age. Syll was always a playful sort of person – lots of fun for kids to be with – especially on the day her brother Amos married Mary Huyard.

While standing off to one side of the bridal table, I noticed how beautiful Syll was as a bridesmaid, seated close to her good friend, Anna Huyard, a sister of the bride. They were *rumspringa* buddies.[14]

---

14 *Rumspringa* is a time for unmarried Amish youth – from ages sixteen to early twenties – to decide who to marry and whether or not to join the church.

Suddenly, I heard Syll's playful voice that was directed at me. "Crawl under the table and sit with us," she was saying.

Getting to Syll wasn't easy in my Sunday attire, but I did it. And what fun I had that night – with all the attention I was getting from people who were stopping by to talk to the bride and groom! It felt like I was back at the farmer's market where I was used to attention from stand holders and customers.

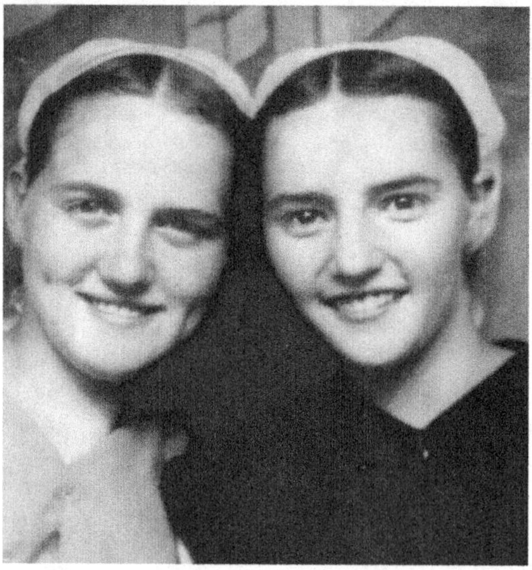

Figure 17: Two good friends, Anna Huyard and Aunt Syll. Taken at a photo booth in downtown Lancaster.

9 | The Farmhouse

Our house on this farm was big, because of several additions appended to the original construction in the 1800s. There was a huge kitchen with a sitting room where Mom's sewing machine was kept, alongside Dad's sofa where he took naps – with Chester on the floor beside him. This Boston Terrier loved my father and followed him around, especially inside the house, where he lived most of the time.

Figure 18: Sisters Priscilla and Susie Ann in roller skates, holding one of the family dogs.

"Chester, Chester," I yelled one evening after supper when the dog was barking at a knock on the front door.

Our painter, also named Chester, was shaking when I opened the door to let him in. He didn't know "what the Harry was going on." He was our regular painter, but hadn't remembered the dog's name.

This house had three doors to the outside which often weren't locked at night. There was a sitting room and a large living room with Amish carpets that covered the wood floor, and were always "taken up" for the church service when it would be held in our home once a year. The house contained two separate basements as well as a big attic which was mostly filled with extra furniture that was nicely stacked. Hickory smoked hams and slabs of bacon hung from the ceiling in the attic – in the winter months, and for our own use. They were smoked to perfection in the smoke house behind the butcher shop, a business shared by Grandpa and Dad.

All this space required much more cleaning than our first house, and it didn't even have the indoor bathroom we had previously enjoyed. Eventually, an addition would be built onto the kitchen which would include a bathroom and a big pantry – but that didn't happen for a year or two. So, my parents used a shower in the basement and we kids took baths in square aluminum tubs.

None of that was a problem since Mom always made sure the basement was warm... but the outhouse in the woodshed was intolerable, especially on cold nights! There were no electric lights and the building was dark and spooky. The flashlights we carried gave off lots of light, but they were always in the way.

Meals were served at the big extension table in the kitchen three times a day. Always at the same time. Plates would be set for our family of six. Plus, the men who worked for Dad and the extras, which included cousins who had dropped in for the day as well as children from the Bronx who stayed a few weeks in the summer, or longer.

Meals and snacks magically appeared for other drop-ins – friends, relatives, and the homeless men (or tramps) who walked the country roads in the summer months, and regularly came to our kitchen door for a hot meal.

The hard luck stories of these road walkers were difficult for a little Amish girl like me to understand. Some had lost their families to alcohol abuse. Others had hit the road after losing their money in the stock market crash of 1929, or after serving in one of the wars. No one talked about Post Traumatic Stress Disorder back then (PTSD, as it is now commonly known), but some of those men may have suffered from it, according to their stories, to which Dad often listened while sitting on a concrete slab in the barn.

A charming sheepherder from the state of New Mexico walked down our farm lane one autumn. He, too, slept in the barn, but ate at our table after Dad hired him to work for a few months. He told stories that made us laugh and always wiped his plate clean with butter bread at the end of every meal.

"You don't have to wash this plate," he'd tell my mother. "It's ready for the next meal."

Mom said, “He probably didn’t want to be a bother,” but she didn’t mind washing his plate along with all the others.

Feeding people at the kitchen table was Dad’s purpose in life and Mom liked it, too. It was fun for them, especially when it was appreciated. Their own kids could be ungrateful, at times, particularly when told to eat everything on our plates. But outsiders like the sheepherder, the road walkers, and the kids from the Bronx were always grateful. They were happy to be part of Mom’s dependable three-meal-a-day routine.

I can’t imagine the cost of food for my parents back then. Even with prices much lower than now. Not just the cost of people food, but also dog food and feed for the farm animals.

We always had several dogs, mostly Boston terriers, and also collies to round up the cows, and always a German shepherd who protected the farm. Road walkers knew not to walk beyond a certain point on our lane when Dad was off somewhere, because a German shepherd would be standing guard. To my knowledge, the dogs never hurt anyone, but they were protective of the family, especially Dad.

These dogs were fun to have around, and they were good playmates for the kids, but I didn’t get attached to pets back then. Occasionally we’d lose one, since they were free to roam around the farm where dangers lurked. Most slept in the barn, but some were house dogs.

Chester had lost one eye to the peck of a chicken, but he died of old age. He took his last breath during a heart attack while lying on the kitchen floor, next to the sofa where Dad was napping. Two other Boston Terriers were killed while chasing cars and trucks. Millie thought she was good at that game, until she, too, was run over after getting caught on a tobacco stalk. The shepherds died of natural death. Rosie, the collie, miraculously recovered from multiple injuries after being run over by the tire of a heavy feed truck. Susie Ann didn't want the vet to put the dog down so she promised to nurse her back to life. Which she did, with the vet's help.

This farm had cats, too. Lots of them, but they were mousers, not house cats. They mostly lived in the barn and the fields, but we'd see them in the cow stable at milking time, waiting for the warm milk Dad poured into a long iron trough. The dogs never drank from that trough, for whatever reason. They had their own feeding bowls.

10 | Endless Work

Variety was the name of the game on our farm. We had a lot of fun, but the work was never done. We just quit at 7:00 in the evening and started all over again at 5:00 in the morning when the roosters crowed, and the cows would stand at the gate behind the barn, waiting to be milked.

Mom's breakfast of eggs, bacon, and mush (or scrapple) made my day, and "coffee soup" was a "must have." Chunks of bread soaked in coffee and sweetened with sugar and milk was God's gift to a kid like me who wasn't as crazy about mornings as I am today.

"This is hard," I'd tell Mom when I'd be tasked with doing something difficult. I hadn't lived on a farm the first six years of my life, so a lot of the chores were new for me. Bottle-feeding the calves with Susie Ann was fun. And I liked helping Mom at the kitchen sink, but the yard was a lot of work and I certainly wasn't ready to milk a cow yet. Not until about age ten or eleven.

Work on that farm was organized. It ebbed and flowed to a daily schedule, dictated by my parents' need for order, school days, the needs of the animals, the weather, and the harvest seasons of the year. Food was plentiful and meals were generously served to most anyone who happened to be in the kitchen at mealtime.

I knew my role in family life and work, and did what had to be done. In between, I read books and entertained dreams of other places, where life wouldn't be so full of physical labor. But there was a daily rhythm and a kind of happiness that kept me going, and on track. There was a reason for being one's very best, which included my parents, teachers, and God who was watching over us.

Dad used to say, "God wants to bless us but we have to do our part," and Mom encouraged us to follow our interests.

Dad taught us to do things that simply had to be done, even when we didn't feel like doing them. Mom was a little different. Although she, too, focused on what had to be done, she also understood the importance of doing things we enjoyed, as much as she liked her sewing machine and other creative projects like gardening, quilting, and cooking.

Mom tried hard to make work fun. She expected us to work together, and promised that we'd have time to play after the work was finished. "Let's do this together," she told us early on. "It's more fun that way and the work gets done faster."

I have fond memories of buffing the big kitchen floor on Saturday mornings after she had wet-mopped and waxed it. One of us would sit on a broom pinned to a cloth while another pulled it all over the floor in our stocking feet, trying hard to throw the rider off. We laughed so hard that our bellies hurt, but that Armstrong linoleum always looked great in the end. Buffed to a lovely shine!

Having fun while we did the physical work was the only way I got through it – it was a life value that stuck.

There were times we'd have to be more quiet. Dad didn't want a lot of fuss in the cow stable during "milking," since the cows would hold their milk if there was too much noise. Other things required quiet too, like feeding the calves and counting the feed bags. Sometimes we'd get noisy at mealtime, but mostly we were well-behaved Amish kids. Dad didn't like a lot of noise during meals, either. Conversation? Yes, but not a lot of "carrying on."

Mom taught us the value of teamwork. It was never one person doing the dishes or going out into the yard to do the work. We did it together, including Mom. She might be pulling weeds in the flower gardens with one or two of us, while others mowed the lawn with a push mower. One of us would push while another pulled with a rope that was tied to the front of the mower. "Sluffing off" wasn't allowed since each kid had to do his share of pushing and pulling. This could be difficult when the blades needed to be sharpened, or the joints of the wheels needed a good squirt of grease.

While growing up, I much preferred my mother's way of doing things, but as I got older, I was thankful for my father's expectations. This, too, was important to my success in life, but I knew in my heart I wasn't going to be a farmer's wife.

Labor on the farm was one of the hardest things I've ever done, but it taught me how to work. I learned to appreciate the "good feelings" that come from getting things done. "Just get it done," I'd say to myself when I was procrastinating with little motivation.

Once a month Dad got a milk check in the mail from the Supplee Milk Company in Philadelphia. It paid the monthly bills in his desk drawer. But, if we were lucky, there would be enough left over for a shopping trip to Rubinson's Department Store – for shoes and clothes –

and maybe a few toys for our collection from Kauffman's Hardware Store across the street.

Most extras, like an additional cow or farm implement were paid with income from the butcher shop, or from cash crops like potatoes or tobacco that were harvested during the summer, and stored in the cool basement of the tobacco shed until prices would increase the following spring due to demand. Other crops like hay, corn, wheat, and straw fed and "bedded down" the farm animals including cows, mules, and horses, along with a few chickens, geese, and ducks.

11 | Fun and Games

Everyone in my family was expected to help with the work on the farm – even at the young age of seven, eight, or nine – but there was always time for fun and games.

Summer treats on the lawn were special. Often, we'd have ice cream after the milking was done, but we had to make it first, using a hand-cranked ice cream maker that transformed the creamy mixture into some of the best ice cream I've eaten. This was not an easy job for us kids, but Dad took over at the end when it was too hard for us to turn. We were dead tired by then, but one mouthful of that vanilla, chocolate, or fresh strawberry ice cream made it all worthwhile.

Ice-cold watermelon was served on the lawn much more often, since that was easier than making ice cream and there was always one cooling in the milk house. Watermelon was my favorite – especially when I was fortunate enough to pick out a nice ripe one from the front porch of Zimmerman's Store, using a technique Dad taught me many years ago.

"Lightly tap it with your fist at several places," he explained as he showed me how to do it. "If you get a hollow sound like this, you know it's a good watermelon."

After the treats, we played games on the front lawn until it got so dark that we couldn't see anything except the stars, the fireflies, and the neighbor's lights in the back part of their house. We would catch the fireflies and watch them light up in a ventilated glass jar for a little while before releasing them.

"Don't let them in there too long. You don't want them to suffocate," Mom would remind us.

We played with our toys and the dogs until bedtime. Or, we sat on the porch with our parents who were relaxing to the country sounds, like the cow bells and the squeaky old windmill that stood tall over the pump house. Wind power pumped most of our water from the well, but it was backed up by a gasoline engine that had its own sounds.

Evenings at our house were different on school days, which started after Labor Day. Playtime after the evening milking would be replaced by school assignments for classes the next day. This homework was done at the big kitchen table, under the bright light of a gasoline lantern, which we kids were told not to touch. I didn't mind that rule since I had seen it "go puff" when Mom put a match to the mantle. I also didn't mess with the pilot light in the propane gas cook stove or the pressure cooker that could hurt me if the lid ever blew its top.

I helped the younger ones with their homework as I was doing my own... trying hard to make time for a quick card game of "snap" or "old maid" before our nine o'clock bedtime. But I couldn't sleep without a bit of reading done under the covers, thanks to the help of a very bright flashlight Mom let me charge to our account at Zimmerman's Hardware Store.

Because we lived without electricity, there were no electric lamps by my bed, or anywhere in the house. The dark of night was meant for sleeping, not reading in bed.

"Go to sleep now," Dad would yell upstairs if he thought maybe I was still reading after nine o'clock. And sometimes he yelled a second time, before retiring to the master bedroom on the first floor, which we knew as the "*commar.*"

On Friday nights, we stayed up a little later to play board games at the kitchen table or to work on projects we kept in a cupboard. There were drawing books, flower-making and embroidery kits, paint-by-number sets and oil paints for making mottos or plaques we hung on our walls. There were metal frames for weaving the potholders we used in the kitchen or sold to friends and neighbors.

Dad often played board games with us, like Parcheesi or Monopoly, which was a challenge since he usually won. He wouldn't give us the game just to make us feel good. We had to earn it.

"Don't give up," Mom would tell us when we'd be tired of losing. "Try, try again."

Monopoly was one of my favorites when I got to be ten or eleven years old. I remember sliding the playing pieces across the board with a passion to win the game that motivated me to "give my all" or "do my best." I took chances buying and selling property that eventually put piles of play money on my side of the board, and I carefully watched the position of the other players. Eventually, I got so good at this game that I won quite frequently, but my interest in real estate never went beyond that game. Real life monopoly would interfere with what I really wanted to be doing!

My parents were social creatures who liked the company of other people. This included family visits that kept us busy, since both came from big families – twelve children on each side and a total of a hundred or so nieces and nephews who were my cousins.

Most lived in Lancaster County back then, but my parents would see some of Dad's family during winter vacations in the Pinecraft section of Sarasota, where my grandparents, Abe and Priscilla Stoltzfus, owned a modest winter home, along with other good friends like Ike and Emma Smoker.[15] Later, after leaving the farm in their early fifties, my parents bought their own vacation house. This was more Dad's idea than Mom's, but she was happy to spend quality time with her sister, Susie (the Glicks from the Maplehof Farm in Quarryville, who were part of this winter scene).

We also spent a great deal of time on Aaron and Ruth Fisher's farm as I was growing up, mostly on alternate Sundays when there was no church service.[16]

Mom and Ruth Fisher were close friends as teenagers and so were Dad and Aaron. The two couples had been married in the same month and had kids the same ages. These marriages might not have happened if the two men had gone west that fall in 1938 (the year they were married). So, for me, it was good that Dad's plan was

---

[15] The Pinecraft community in Sarasota has been a favorite vacation spot for Amish snowbirds since it was first established, sometime during the 1950s. It's a vacation spot for social creatures from cold winter states like Indiana, Ohio, Pennsylvania, and Maryland, or a second home for retirees who stay for the "snowbird season" from November-April.

[16] Amish church service was held every other Sunday, leaving the alternate Sunday for visiting relatives and friends, which was usually a full-day affair including a noon meal.

thwarted by Grandma who, as you'll recall, burned his driver's license.

The Fishers lived on a farm – north of Strasburg, on Route 741, which was close to an hour-long buggy ride for us. There were always games for the kids and meals and snacks the whole day.

In the summer, we kids played outdoor games like *baseball* and *kick the can,* but in the winter we were limited to board games in the house, or to *bag tag* we played on the second floor of their barn. Throwing a knotted-up part of an empty feed bag at each other was lots of fun, but I was careful to avoid the cobwebs that got in my hair and the "way up high rafters" that were a bit too wobbly for my "scaredy-cat" tendencies.

Playing on any of those rafters was dangerous, like crossing the Lincoln Highway East in a buggy, or driving over the railroad tracks at the original Gordonville Crossing where the big steam engines were known to run over things and people that got in the way.

Those dangers could not totally be avoided if we wanted to do fun things like visiting the Fishers, but we had to be careful not to get hurt. Dad always played it safe by leading our horse, Will, across the railroad tracks, just in case he might get spooked to something strange, like a noisy train coming up the tracks at high speed, or a loud steam whistle in the distance.

Dad would often mention "Uncle Joe" as we approached the Gordonville Railroad Crossing, or when we'd hear the loud whistle of a steam engine from our house at certain times of the day.

"There goes Uncle Joe," Dad would say with a pleased look on his face. "He's on time again."

Joe was actually one of Grandma's younger uncles who never joined the Amish Church and worked on the Pennsylvania Railroad (PRR) for about forty years, as an engineer running fast passenger and commuter trains. He was a role model or a "celebrity of sorts" to Grandma's extended family and his hometown of Gordonville, even after he was given a ninety-day suspension and a demotion that cut his retirement pay. It seems this "Fast Dutchman" (as he was known) was driving too fast that day, when his train derailed, causing a wreck.[17] But he and his wife, Maggie, did retire well on their farm in Gordonville, and Joe passed away when I was fifteen years old.

Joe's interest in becoming an engineer had been sparked at age seven, during a long train ride from Kansas to Pennsylvania. The engineer driving that train had taken a liking to this little Amish boy who asked a lot of questions, and invited him to sit in the cab for much of the trip to blow the whistle and even operate a few of the controls.[18]

This train ride inspired Joe to get a job on the railroad tracks in his teenaged years, determined to become an engineer, which back then, was "looked up to," much like today's airline pilots.

---

[17] Stoltzfus, Sam. (2016). *The History of the Village of Gordonville.* Gordonville, PA: Pud Sam Press, pp. 9-10.

[18] Fisher, Gideon and Elizabeth (Stoltzfus). (1979). *An Early Move to Kansas.* Gordonville, PA: Gordonville Print Shop, p.11.

Daytrips in the summer months were lots of fun for us, and Holloway Beach in Charlestown, Maryland, was a favorite. After being in a car for an hour or so, we kids ate a light picnic lunch, jumped off diving boards, ate hot dogs from the food stands, and floated on big truck innertubes we brought with us (deflated, of course).

We laughed and carried on as Mom took us out to where our feet didn't touch bottom. Many days we ended up with a sunburn that hurt on the drive home. Mom rubbed lotion on the red spots, which didn't help much, but we soon learned to cover our skin with higher levels of protection to avoid sunburn and melanoma.

Every daytrip was a little different, which included the miniature train display at Roadside America and the gardens at Nolt's Fish Farm, Star® Roses, and Longwood Gardens. Being around the beauty of those places broadened our horizons and always inspired us to take home a few ideas and products to spruce up our own living spaces.

The Farmers' Fairs in New Holland and Ephrata were fun, too. The streets in the center of town were closed off for these fairs, which started with an opening day parade. They continued on with things like animal shows and sales, tractor competitions, carnival rides for the kids, and lots of "yummy junk food" like hot dogs, funnel cakes, and pink cotton candy that melted in our mouth.

Women took their best cakes, pies, and floral arrangements to the fair, and children proudly brought their biggest pumpkin or a farm animal they had raised, hoping for first or second prize that would get their names in the local newspapers.

Summer trips to the mountains of Potter County, Pennsylvania, were much-deserved vacations for my family. I especially remember a particular weekend trip to Coudersport, where we stayed in a rustic cabin owned by a hunting camp where Uncle Mel was a member.

In order for us to get away, Dad's brother Dan was put in charge of the milking for the four-day weekend, while we spent time with Mel and his beautiful fiancée Ada Ruth (who were Mennonite). She was so pretty I kept staring at her, seeing how much in love she was with my uncle. She liked me too, even at twelve years old, in my Amish clothes.

Mel was Mom's youngest brother – the most handsome one of the bunch – driving a new car that weekend, with a very bright spotlight that was great for "spotting deer" in their natural environment.

"I'll see if I can get any closer," Mel said one night as he coasted down the hill with the headlights off, to the place where we could see a big buck in the woods with a rack to be proud of, along with two fawns and a doe, all eyes looking straight ahead.

"Look at them!" I screamed, with special attention to the babies that stayed close to their mama. "They're adorable."

These wild creatures stood in the woods by a mountain road, staring at the bright light aimed right at them. I wondered how they survived in those places, especially in the cold winter months. I had read *Bambi,* who I bonded with, but there was so much I didn't know about deer back then. I didn't understand their habit of eating everything in sight when there's an over-population, or when there's not enough rain to water "the stuff" they eat in the wild.

The men in my family were hunters, which included trips to the mountains for deer and wild turkey. Pheasants and rabbits were plentiful at home, and Mom could de-feather, skin, and cook any of it in a very short time. The pigeons in the barn and the ducks and geese by the spring in our meadow were part of this scene too, and so was duck hunting on Uncle Sam and Aunt Mary's farm in Chestertown, Maryland.[19]

This wild game was "good eating," but I preferred fish from the seafood truck that came to our farm once a week, and the fresh rockfish Dad would bring home from chartered fishing trips to Rock Hall, Maryland. Or the fresh trout caught in the cold mountain streams of Coudersport, especially when it was served the same day.

"This is sooo good," I told Uncle Mel after the first bite or two. "Is there more?" He chuckled, letting me know there was much more. All I could eat.

Mel was our cook that weekend, along with my mother who had brought a lot of food with us, in the trunk of the car. It was quite obvious that she loved doing things with her youngest brother whom she had helped raise as one of the older sisters.

She was happy about his plans to marry Ada Ruth Umble that fall, who always felt more like a sister than a sister-in-law. And, Mom felt the same about Ruth Metz who would marry her brother, Ike, a year later.

These two brothers chose not to stay Amish, but Mom was quite happy with the Mennonite women they married. "They fit in the family."

---

[19] This family had moved to Cecil County, Maryland, in the 1950s, when the Amish in Lancaster County were solicited by banks and the Chamber of Commerce – for their farming skills.

That hunting cabin in Coudersport was like many others scattered along the main roads or perched on the side of a mountain. Quite rustic, it was still equipped with a useful kitchen designed for the hunters who ate all, or most, of their meals at this place, perhaps staying up late to play games, or compete on the well-used archery board attached to the wall.

Archery kept me occupied for hours that weekend, sparking my interest in the sport. But there were also board games, including Monopoly, which I was good at. It was my "ace in the hole" that weekend, but I was also in good shape to hike Baldy Mountain behind our cabin, and run down the hill since there were no trees.

I was a fast runner in those days – skinny as a rail. Following me down that hill wasn't easy for my two little sisters, who were trying to keep up. In fact, they couldn't stop. Chubby little Priscilla lost her balance, and down she went, on her knees (and forehead). We had nothing to treat the bruises except a little water from a bottle Mom was carrying. So, Dad picked Priscilla up and carried her back to the cabin. She was crying by then, mostly scared, I think. The bruises did get cleaned up and treated, to the point where we thought she'd be okay, but Priscilla wasn't happy. Her "ouchies" hurt.

The outhouse in that cabin was a bit scary at night because of the bears that showed up at the garbage cans. But we kids didn't go out there without adult supervision, a flashlight, and something noisy to chase the bears away. There were rifles in the cabin in case we needed them.

12 | Farm Experiences

I loved those trips to the mountains and beaches, but the farm was my day-to-day reality. "Girl work" in the house and garden was a lot more appealing to me than "boy work" in the barn and fields, but I had both experiences as I got a little older.

Aunt Syll was no longer working for Mom after she got married, a few months before my eleventh birthday. So, I helped Mom more after that and finally I milked a cow – as a learning experience. My roles developed when I turned twelve and thirteen, but Mom set a few limits. She didn't allow us girls to do heavy work in the fields that might hurt our chances to have babies.

Those limits were fine with me, since I didn't want to throw heavy bales of hay and straw onto the farm wagons in the fields, nor did I want the gummy job of spearing tobacco on a hot summer day. I wasn't interested in mucking out stables or driving the four-mule team in the fields. But I enjoyed the camaraderie of sorting and bagging baskets full of potatoes that were brought in from the fields, where the potato pickers were filling up the baskets.

Cousin Dave (Aunt Sadie's kid) and I would be in the barn that day, standing on either side of a machine, known as the potato sorter. Our job was to pick off bad potatoes as they came across the belt of the sorter, and before they dropped into a bag of remaining good potatoes for the dealers. Some of the potatoes, if they had three or more eyes, would be put into a basket, to be cut up into sections for next year's planting. We had to work fast and stay alert since the belt kept moving, but we loved that job and we'd laugh and have fun. He was paid and I wasn't.

I didn't have an allowance, but I could ask for what I wanted as long as it was reasonable. If I wanted money, I'd work for it. Uncle Ben would pay me $15.00 to wash and wax his car, by hand, which wasn't easy, and took a good part of the day. I also babysat his daughters when I was 12 and 13, and later worked for him at the motel when I was in college. Sometimes my sisters and I would peddle sweet corn and other garden vegetables to our town neighbors, and we'd get to keep some of the cash.

Pulling tobacco (grown from seeds under muslin) was a fun job too – done in teams. We kids would throw wet tobacco plants at each other until we were told not to, and squirt each other with the water hose. Planting tobacco with my parents was even more fun, in a mindless and routine kind of way. I can still hear the *ding-ding* of the bell on that planter and the "gush of water" from the tank that let Mom and I know exactly when to drop each of the young plants into the rows made by the rig that Dad was driving. We tried hard to do it right so we wouldn't have to walk through the field another time to fix our mistakes. Replanting tobacco in the hot sun, with handheld tools and a bucket full of water was no fun at all. We hated the job.

Dad would remind us to "do things right the first time so you don't have to do it over."

There was something I liked about the smell of cured tobacco that hung in our tobacco barn. Perhaps it reminded me of the family camaraderie on cold winter Saturdays (or evenings) – in the stripping room, where we pulled the leaves off the stalks before they were baled and sold to the local buyers as cigar tobacco. But that could be a tiresome job too, especially at the end of the season.

I've learned to explain the phrase "stripping room," since many do not know its meaning, as the Amish farmers in Lancaster County understand it. This misunderstanding actually happened while Mom's brother, Leroy, was trying to have a conversation with a young Amish girl – Lucy, from Goshen, Indiana – who he later married.

Lucy had been a guest at my parents' wedding that frigid day in December, when Leroy suggested they "get out of the cold, and warm up in the stripping room." The look he got from Lucy was priceless. It prompted him to explain that this space is where the tobacco leaves are stripped off the stalks and baled before selling them to the local tobacco buyers. He told her, "There's a stove in that room that is always kept on during cold weather like now."

"Tobacco is a nasty thing," Pud Sam Stoltzfus, reminded me. "Most of our men don't smoke or chew like they used to, which is good. A few of the 'diehards' still grow it as a cash crop, but businesses have pretty much taken its place." His wife, Katie mentioned that women in her culture never smoked in her lifetime, but she'd heard stories about women a long time ago who smoked a crudely rolled-up tobacco leaf. She thinks this was done by other farm women back then, not just the Amish.

Dad smoked cigars as I was growing up, but that stopped in his thirties when a doctor found a dark spot on his lungs. He tried chewing tobacco as an alternative, but not for long after Mom stepped into the situation. She hated that dirty habit and warned that she would put something nasty into his tobacco pouch if he didn't quit.

He was surprised when it actually happened, and as a germaphobe, it "groused him out."

"I warned you," she said, with a silly smile on her face, "but you didn't think I'd do it."

Dad liked growing tobacco and most anything else. He enjoyed the challenge of bringing out the best in whatever he grew and showing it off. This included the farm crops, the garden vegetables, and the twenty or so rose bushes in our front yard that thrived on water he mixed with horse manure and sprayed with a chemical-free laundry soap.

The blooms on those rose bushes were gorgeous – in many colors, which we kept picking up on our day trips to Star® Roses retail store in Chester County. I loved those gardens as did my parents, so the trips were frequent, always requiring a hired driver.

Mom loved gardening – all kinds. She enjoyed the vegetables and berries she grew every year and the grapevines that grew on the fence by our house. I still remember the loving way she cut the grape clusters from those vines with scissors, carefully placing them into a basket until she was ready to turn them into grape juice for the winter months. I liked eating those concord grapes right from the vines and was always sorry to see the season end.

Gardening was never something I enjoyed doing by myself, but I liked the camaraderie of helping my parents, and the stuff I got to eat right there in the garden where everything tasted so very good.

I enjoyed horses and ponies back then, although I was a bit scared of them – especially of the Belgian field horses on my grandparents' farm in Buena Vista. I'd follow Mom's brothers to the stables where the horses were fed and groomed, and I'd watch them get hitched up to the wagons and farm implements. But I always stood off to the side, careful not to be stepped on by those huge hooves with the bushy white hair in the back.

I wasn't scared of our carriage horse, Will, who was too old to do anything bad. But I never hitched him up to the carriage. Nor did I ask Mom for the reins when I'd be sitting in the front seat of the buggy with her.

Yet I always had a secret wish for a pony, knowing it would never happen – not even at Christmas. The books and clothes I asked for would be nicely wrapped on Christmas morning, but never a pony. Dad thought they were dangerous for kids and he didn't want us around them.

"Children get hurt by horses and ponies," he kept saying as he reminded me of the accidents in his family – and Mom's. It was her brother, Amos, as you may remember, who was killed by a team of horses that backed a farm wagon into the side of the barn where he was standing.

Dad's younger brother, Ben, had been badly hurt as a teenager while riding bareback at top speed. Apparently, he was thrown forward over the horse's head when it stopped abruptly, for no apparent reason. Surgeries were required and Uncle Ben spent a year or so in and out of hospitals, often confined to a wheelchair and a hospital bed in the kitchen.

Grandpa's medical bills must have been high at that time – during the Great Depression – but fortunately Ben recovered and was able to work. He would always have a limp and a bit of discomfort, but at least he lived.

I would have been a fool not to admit the dangers involved with horses and ponies, but I missed out on a physical kind of self-confidence I've seen in children who learned how to ride a pony or drive a carriage horse.

My childhood friend, Barbie Esh, was confident with horses. "I could handle a horse or a team of mules at age twelve like a grownup and Dad let me do it," she proudly told me.

Her Uncle Aaron thought she was too young to be driving her father's fast carriage horses on the road, but Barbie's dad, Jake Esh, knew she was capable. He saw her control of the horses and the mule team she drove in the fields.

Obviously, Barbie wasn't a "scaredy cat" like me when it came to physical challenges. She was also assertive in getting her father's permission to drive the carriage horses and the mules at a time when he needed her help. She managed to have something similar to the pony I wished for – but never got, not even at Christmas.

Figure 19: Barbie Esh (age 12) driving the horse carriage.

Instead, there would be a shopping trip to New Holland a week or so before Christmas Day, where we kids would choose one special Christmas gift from Kauffman's Hardware Store or Rubinson's Department Store across the street. We'd pick out things like a doll, scooter, express wagon, roller skates, ice skates, a music box, or a sled along with a few family gifts, like games, balls, accessories for the playroom, etc.

It always seemed like my little brother got more toys and games from Kauffman's than we girls did, but we got more from Rubinson's across the street. They had pretty dolls and doll accessories for my little sisters and clothes for me, which usually included a pair of shoes and a few other things I may have wanted. But there was always "just one" of each. Never two sweaters, two pairs of shoes, or even two candy bars.

"You only need one," Mom would tell us and she lived by that same standard.

On Christmas morning, the wrapped gifts would sit by Mom's sewing machine, where the Kris Kindli (the Christ Child) had dropped them off the night before Christmas – through an unlocked window. The cookies we had left for him were gone by then and the window was locked. I knew this wasn't real, but it was a fun fantasy, just like Santa Claus. I imagined Kris Kindli, with wings, flying through glass windows like an angel, leaving gifts and eating cookies, while Santa Claus had to deal with reindeer that were never meant to fly.

We spent the rest of the day at home – playing with our games and toys, or reading the books Mom had picked up for me on one of her shopping trips to Lancaster City. Dinner was a big deal, served at noon. There was always a turkey and stuffing, prepared the Amish Way, as "*roascht.*" The kitchen table was spruced up with a white tablecloth, a handmade centerpiece, and a few of my favorite foods that were served on Mom's "good dishes" from the Ebersol china cupboard.

A dish of fresh fruit would sit by my plate as an appetizer, and a red and green Jello salad layered with Philadelphia cream cheese – shaped like a Christmas tree – stood out among the side dishes of creamed corn, mashed potatoes, a green bean casserole and candied sweet potatoes. Dessert was often one of Mom's unbelievably good pecan pies, along with a nice assortment of cookies and candies the gals in my family always made for this special holiday season, which took several days.

The homemade candy was a favorite, like the chocolate candy bars mixed with caramel and peanuts, chocolate covered pretzels, and peanut butter crackers, along with the taffy we had pulled until it was hard enough to cut into small pieces and wrap in waxed paper.

Most of these treats were stored in a cold room until Christmas Day, but Mom usually gave in to our pleas for a few pieces here or there. Maybe she remembered that her brother, Amos, hadn't gotten to eat the chocolate candy one Christmas, because of the fatal accident the day before.

Figure 20: Making the Christmas candy. Mom and Eva pulling taffy.

13 | The Last Sleepover

Summer sleepovers on my grandparents' farm in Buena Vista were special occasions. This was a time for me to be alone with my mother's parents.

I was twelve or thirteen when the last one took place at the end of the summer, soon after my grandparents moved to the *Daudy haus* to start their retirement years. But the sleepovers had begun many years earlier for me, when I was just five or six, back in the farmhouse when most of Mom's brothers and sisters were still living there at home.

A postcard from Mommy always came in the mail when the time was right for a sleepover. She would tell my mother what day and time Daudy would pick me up at the bus stop in the little town of White Horse. When the bus pulled up in front of the general store, Daudy would be standing at the railing by his horse, which was not always tied. He was never late.

Nothing had changed much when I got off the bus for the very last sleepover. Daudy was standing by his horse, talking to the locals. "This is my oldest grandchild," he told these neighbors. "She's Lizzie's daughter." As we drove away in the spring wagon, he told me how tall I'd grown, and wanted to know what I'd been doing. He teased me about the chocolate smear on the front of my dress. "Is it a Hershey's chocolate bar with almonds?" he asked, knowing that was my favorite.

On our way to their house, we stopped to see his sister, Katie Beiler, who had several daughters, including Anna who was my age. We didn't see each other very often, but we had a lot of fun when we were together, during our summer vacations from school.

As kids, Anna and I had entertained ourselves with stick horses, dolls, paper cutouts from the Sears catalog, and pretend games that reflected our culture. We hopped around on stilts or tin cans tied to sturdy ropes, rode scooters, and played ball games like *kalyover*. Skinned knees and stubbed toes were common occurrences during those visits, but we knew we'd soon be feeling better thanks to the methylate or mercurochrome that was painted on our "ouchies."

Most of Katie's daughters had black hair and dark eyes I admired. Mom was dark too, but I looked more like the light-complexioned cousins on my father's side of the family. Anna was pale-skinned as well. The dark hair and dark eyes in Mom's family have long been a mystery to me, since the *Christian Fisher Family (Book of Descendents, 1957)* has both sides of my Lapp and Stoltzfus family falling into a long line of Swiss-German ancestors who came to America in the mid 1700s.[20]

Mom's brown eyes seemed exceptionally dark and piercing when we kids were misbehaving, or when she didn't like something that was going on. She never laid a hand on us or used mean words, but that cross look in her eyes always worked in her favor. We didn't know what

---

[20] Fisher, John M. Family. (1957). *Christian Fisher Family*. Ronks, PA: Amos Fisher.

might happen next if we didn't "straighten up," nor did we want to find out. We also wanted to please her.

On the second day of the sleepover, I expected to wake up in the morning to a breakfast of eggs and bacon, or ham, and maybe a piece of jelly bread. My grandparents would have coffee, but there would be no coffee soup for me since that tradition had come from my father's side of the family.

The three of us put our "paddies under the table" for a minute or so of silent prayer before we started eating, and again at the end of the meal before Mommy and I left the table to wash the dishes. This was a time for us to thank God for all his blessings, which included the food and those who prepared it.

My father used to say, "God wants to bless us," and my mom reminded us to be thankful. A grateful attitude about things would make us feel better than the constant complaining that was easy to fall into. That was Mom's thinking. She also believed in God's protection, which included his angels. I knew what she meant, because of that framed print that hung in my bedroom of a little girl being caught by an angel as she was falling off a bridge.

After breakfast on that second day, Mommy and I would walk to her big garden, across the driveway in front of her house. We'd pick a vegetable for the evening meal, and maybe a quart or two of blueberries, raspberries, or strawberries. Of course, I would pop a few big, warm, juicy ones into my mouth as we walked along the rows, and if I was lucky, I'd find a few hull peas ready to eat, right there in the garden. They're best that way!

Daudy would be getting the horse ready for our trip to the Gap National Bank, Rhoades General Store, and maybe Mose Lapp's shoe repair shop. He'd hitch up the horse to the spring wagon after it was fed and groomed. Then, before we'd take off, that horse would get an apple, a few pats on the neck, and a pinch or two of chewing tobacco meant to keep the worms out of its intestines.

I remember being hoisted onto the wagon seat as Daudy gripped the lines with one hand and pulled himself up from the hub. Then he'd cluck at the horse and lightly tap him with the reins. "Giddyup," he'd say, as we headed down the long, hilly farm lane to Buena Vista Road. I'd smile up at him and he'd smile back before spitting tobacco juice off to the side.

Was I really safe in that spring wagon or did I just feel safe? It was open like the rumble seat cars. There were no seat belts, but Daudy's big hand would come over in front of me when he saw any kind of danger. He was protective and his eyes would twinkle when he was teasing. I liked that about him.

Daudy kept his foot on the brake ever so lightly as we went down the hill. He didn't want the weight of the wagon pushing against the horse. He was protective of that animal as well, and I know he really liked him.[21]

At five-thirty on the second day of my last sleepover, the three of us had just finished the evening meal and were sitting in the kitchen. Mommy was darning socks

---

[21] That horse also took good care of Daudy as he got older. He knew to take the buggy home when his master fell asleep and, fortunately, there were no accidents. People in that neighborhood watched out for the horse and driver as they traveled those back-country roads that weren't as busy as they are now. I remember Mom being concerned about Daudy's safety in that buggy as he got older, but she agreed with Aunt Miriam's decision not to take the horse away from him.

and I was enjoying one of the travel magazines Daudy kept on a shelf, alongside his favorite novel, *Rosanna of the Amish,* written by Joseph W. Yoder. This was one of the first novels I read as a child, along with *Heidi*, but I mostly read biographies of famous women back then, and a few men I admired. I also read every Nancy Drew book in the bookmobile truck that came to our school, and most of the Hardy Boys detective series.

Daudy liked reading too, which I saw on sleepovers. I'd see him sitting at the kitchen table, reading a Lancaster newspaper and one of the Amish publications like the *Sugarcreek Budget,* which was filled with letters and poems written by some of the Amish he knew from his travels.

The mantle clock on the shelf above his head would tick off the minutes, telling us when it was bedtime. But, before going to bed, the three of us would kneel up to the sofa and chairs at the far end of the kitchen, while Daudy read a prayer in German from a little book, which was probably the "*Gebet.*" Then I would climb up the steps to one of the guest rooms on the second floor.

It was warm up there because there were no fans or air-conditioning, but I felt a nice breeze coming in through the old-fashioned removable screens in the bedroom window, which reminded me of home. This triggered a bit of homesickness, but I soon fell asleep to the squeaky old water wheel cable as it moved back and forth... across the front side of the house, under my bedroom window.

I was ready to go home the next day on the White Horse bus. But I would always remember the soothing sound of that water wheel cable, and the farm in Buena Vista where I could read until I didn't want to do it anymore. There was never enough time at home for all the reading I wanted to do.

14 | A Sudden Awakening

Mom got sick one winter, close to my thirteenth birthday. No one knew the pain she was having in her stomach. Nor did we know the stress she was under, until we almost lost her.

I don't know what made me look over my shoulder at Mom that cold winter night when we kids were doing our homework at the kitchen table. She was slumped over in a chair by the coal stove, white as a ghost, with a blanket wrapped around her shivering shoulders.

"Mom, you're bleeding!" I yelled in desperation as I pointed to the pool of blood at her feet, partially covered by the blanket. "Dad, look!"

"Take care of things here," Dad said as he got up from his place at the table and grabbed a coat from a hook behind the stove. "I'll be back soon," he yelled, as he rushed to the front door. "Mamm needs an ambulance. I'm going up to Brackie's to use their phone."

I was terrified at the thought of losing my mother, but also relieved when the Gordonville Ambulance crew arrived and took over. Right about that same time, Dad was back at the house with his hired driver, Manny Nafzinger, who would take him to the emergency room of Lancaster General Hospital.

"Keep this kerosene light on low and take the kids to our bed," Dad instructed as he put a match to the wick, and extinguished the bright gasoline lantern that hung above the kitchen table.

"I won't be long," he said as he rushed out the front door to Manny's car.

I had just been put in charge of my sisters and brother, who were ten, eight, and six, so I did my best to address their fears and explain the situation. I couldn't share my own anxiety since I was in charge, so I tried hard to stay calm as we jumped into my parents' bed, snuggled up, and waited for Dad to come home.

I couldn't sleep that night, even after getting to my own bed. I was so worried about my mother. The next day, we stayed home from school, but I remember little of what happened, except that Aunt Syll was brought in to help. She was married by then and had two children, so she probably didn't stay overnight, due to her own family responsibilities, but I don't remember the details.

Syll explained that Mom had lost a great deal of blood from a bleeding stomach ulcer and might not make it, even though most of her eight brothers had donated all of the type AB blood she desperately needed. I fell into Syll's arms and cried my heart out, before running upstairs to my bedroom.

"God, please, don't let my mother die," I pleaded in desperation as I fell on the bed, face down. "Please, I'll do anything you want if you let her live. I will wear those heavy black stockings to church without complaining... and the white organdy cape and apron, too."

Bargaining with God was the only thing I knew to do with the horrible news that I might lose my mother. I had always been an independent child, but Mom was my emotional rock. She was the family cheerleader, always encouraging us to keep going and expect the best.

Fear of losing her triggered my first epiphany. I suddenly needed God but didn't know much about him back then except that he was a "*Gute Mann*" (good man) who wanted the best for me. I also knew that he didn't bless kids who told lies or took things that didn't belong to them, and that he could see everything that was happening. I couldn't hide anything.

A day or two later Dad told us Mom was going to be okay. A third of her stomach had been removed because of the bleeding ulcer but she would be coming home soon. "Mamm is very weak," he said in Pennsylvania Dutch. "She will need a lot of help from all of us."

I don't remember her homecoming, but I did help a lot more after that – and I stopped complaining about the clothes I had to wear to church. But I always took off the white organdy cape and apron as soon as I could, since they were uncomfortable, and full of straight pins holding the pieces together.

Mom was sympathetic to my complaints about those whites, since she hadn't had to wear them in her youth. But Mom couldn't change my situation. It was simply the way things were done in our church district – and the bishop's wife, Phenie, enforced the rules.

I was somewhat afraid of Aunt Phenie who watched me like a hawk, or so I thought. I'd often see her staring at me when I wasn't sitting perfectly still during a three and a half hour church service, or when I'd eat candy from a pocket under my apron. I remember a time when I was little, maybe five years old, and she chased me home with a broom, after I had been throwing small pebbles at the closed wooden shutters of her house that faced our garden. She obviously hadn't realized that I wasn't trying to be bad at that age; I just liked the sound.

"*Schick dich*" (Behave yourself), Mom had said when I told her about the chase. "Be nice to her."

Mom always described Aunt Phenie as *different,* which I also heard from others. She wasn't as kind as other Amish women I knew and she seemed angry about something.

From my experience, I assumed Phenie didn't like children, but later I learned that she had given birth to three stillborn infants within three years. Her only son, who was badly crippled, had died the year I was born. She did have two grown step-daughters from Uncle Dan's previous marriage, which was nice, but she wanted her own children.

"No woman should have to bear such pain," I said to myself as tears came to my eyes one day as I thought about her unfortunate circumstances. My resentment toward Aunt Phenie quickly turned to compassion, so I guess I was ready to let that resentment go.

Fortunately, Mom recovered from the ulcer. About a half-year later, she offered me a deal I couldn't resist. "Why don't you make breakfast in the morning and I'll go out to milk?" she suggested. "I'm ready to do something different and it will give me a chance to work with your father in the mornings."

I accepted, of course, and my life got better when I no longer had to get up at 5:00 A.M. to milk the cows and clean up the milk house. The new arrangement was great and Mom liked it, too. It was a win-win, but I continued to do the barn work at 5:00 in the afternoon. I was doing much more work for Mom after her recovery, but there were times I wasn't as helpful as I could have been.

At age thirteen, I still had a lot of kid in me, which was evident when Dad hired "Squirrely's son," Amos, a second cousin of mine who needed a job after completing the eighth grade in our local public school.

Dad had agreed to the father's request to "give Amos two meals a day and a hundred dollars a month, and teach him how to work since he hadn't grown up on a farm."

Amie did learn a lot from Dad, but he wasn't done playing yet either, by the looks of the black shoe marks we kids put around the kitchen table while Mom was out milking in the morning.[22]

---

[22] The night before Dad's funeral in 2002, I was surprised to see Amos and his wife, Hannah, waiting in line to offer their condolences. "You two have come a long way for this," I said, knowing they lived in Chestertown, Maryland. "I wouldn't have missed this for anything," Amie replied. "I'm here to pay my respects to the man who taught me how to work. I owe my success to him." After working for my father for a year or so, Amie had moved on, to learn carpentry. This led him to create his own business as a building contractor, which included waterfront properties in Cecil and Chester Counties, Maryland.

Part III

Leaving the Amish

15 | Our Church District

The church service held that fateful day on the Push Esh farm was one of many I had attended since I was a baby on up.

People would come together for these services every other week; the location rotated among member families so no one would need to host more than once a year.

Living room carpets would be taken up a week or so before the day of the service and the house would get a good cleaning. A fully enclosed wagon filled with backless benches would get delivered to its usual place behind the barn, and the benches would be set up in the first floor of the house the day before. Neighbors would help.

My parents were members of the Intercourse Church district, which included about 30-40 families, who lived in our neighborhood. Many were related to us – my grandparents, Aunt Sadie's family, and the families of Grandpa's brothers. His youngest brother, Stef, had been ordained as one of the ministers when I was just six years old, and of course his other brother, Uncle Dan, was the bishop.

This church district was one of many in the Old-Order Amish Settlement of Lancaster County, established circa 1801. The settlement was (and still is), the oldest existing of its kind, scattered throughout the United States and Canada. Also, the most prosperous.

It traces its beginnings to Christian Fisher, an Amish bishop, who relocated his family from the Wyomissing area of Berks County to farms in the Mascot/Stumptown area of Lancaster County, a few miles east of Lancaster City.[23]

Christian was a grandson of Nicolas Stoltzfus whose family had settled in Berks County after sailing across the Atlantic Ocean on *Ship Polly*, arriving in Philadelphia in 1766.[24]

Nicolas was a German immigrant, raised by Lutheran parents on a farm they owned in Zweibrucken, Germany. He married a young Amish girl, Anna Elizabeth Bachman, whose people had been persecuted for their radical Anabaptist Christian beliefs against infant baptism and service in the military. Nicolas wanted to get away from the dictates of the German government and the official Lutheran Church, which forbade him to stay on the family land, after he married the Amish girl.[25] It seems the Amish were not allowed to own land in certain districts, because of their radical beliefs.

Land ownership was very important to Nicolas and other Anabaptist Christians[26] in the 1700s, since it was a big part of their European farm culture. Many aspired to

---

[23] Fisher, Amos L. (1957). *Descendants and History of the Christian Fisher Family*. Ronks, PA: self-published, p. 33.

[24] Stoltzfus, Levi L. (1986). *Revealed Life of Nicolas Stoltzfus*. Morgantown, PA: Masthof Press, p. 9.

[25] Ibid., pp. 7-9.

[26] Anabaptists: Amish, Mennonites, Brethren, and Hutterites.

something better than the work they were doing as highly-skilled tenant farmers in the agricultural areas of Germany, Switzerland, France and The Netherlands. So, it's not surprising that they risked the perils of sailing across the Atlantic in extremely overcrowded ships, never to see their family or friends again.

Food was scarce on those sailboats, often including rats and mice. Starvation was common and many died on those voyages.[27] These non-resistant, peace-loving Amish folks may also have been surprised and shocked by the problems they faced in the new world. Land had to be cleared of its trees and brush before it could be farmed, and their Native American neighbors were often quite aggressive since their territory – sold by William Penn at a low price – was constantly being invaded.[28] However, the Amish moved ahead in spite of those odds, with great hopes that their children and grandchildren would have a better life in Pennsylvania.

---

[27] Fisher, Amos L. (1957). *Descendants and History of Christian Fisher Family*. Ronks, PA: self-published, pp. 6-7.

[28] Ibid., pp. 11-18.

16 | The Ex-communication

The Eshes were good neighbors. Our farms connected in the back fields, but there were other connections, too. We liked each other and always got along. There was never a bad word between us, and obvious respect on both sides. "What happened that day was sad," Push Esh once told me. "Your father and grandfather are good people... good farmers... good businessmen."

It seems that some people didn't quite know what to think about the violations in Ike Smoker's elevator factory, so they didn't take sides at the special church meeting in the spring of 1954. Others – like the men in my family – stood up for their good friend Ike. They saw the value of his hay elevator that was selling like 'hotcakes' in the farm belts of the U.S. and Canada and they wanted Bishop Dan to "let Ike alone to run his business, changing the rules, if necessary."

But another group of men pressured Bishop Dan to enforce the existing rules, no matter what. New things were happening in that machine shop (or factory) and "what might this lead to," they wondered. "It has to be stopped. It can't go on!"

These violations included forklifts, a generator to run the welders, and telephones and electricity that had been installed under the name of a business partner who was not Amish. All of these doings were against church rules back then, and had not yet been approved by the bishops in our Lancaster County Amish settlement.

Ike Smoker wasn't going to be pressured by the bishop into selling his thriving business that was making money "hand over fist." He had put a lot of sweat and equity into his company, which included loans, and proceeds from the farm he had sold before starting this business. Now, the factory was growing quickly, and Ike was on a roll! The hay elevator he had invented was seen by many as a revolutionary piece of equipment, badly needed by farmers. His vision was coming true! His invention was the next step to New Holland Machine Company's hay baler, which was also selling like hotcakes on the international market.

Bishop Dan would have the final word on this issue. As an Amish bishop, ordained by God, he had total authority to handle it as he saw fit. He would announce his final decision at this meeting, where two or three ministers were attending, and some say the decision had already been made. This wasn't the first time this issue was being discussed. There had been at least one other special meeting after church – two weeks before the ex-communication.[29]

[29] Fisher, Benuel M. (2017). *Beyond the Crossroads:* Fisher Publishing, 772-A Peters Road, New Holland, PA 17557, pp. 148-150.

Church had gone on as usual that morning – at least before the special meeting began at noon. We were inside a large farmhouse, filled with backless benches and perhaps a few chairs or rockers for the older folks.

The service had lasted for three and a half hours before dismissal. Typically, we'd eat lunch right away, on two very long tables. Men would be served first. This meant the women and children had to wait for the men to come out of the meeting. Then after the men had been served, women and children could finally eat. Never before... and no exceptions. Not even that day. "It's just the way things are done."

The menfolk in the special meeting sat on benches, and a dozen or so were seated on a separate bench. These few fathers and their grown sons were openly showing support for their good friend, Ike, and his fast-growing elevator company.

Both sides had their arguments, but Bishop Dan would soon be making the final decision. By all reports, tempers were hot.

"You either must sell your business or I'm going to have to ex-communicate you," Bishop Dan finally told Ike Smoker.

But before Ike Smoker could respond, a loud voice spoke up from the opposition bench. "If you ex-communicate Ike, you ex-communicate all of us."

I imagine a hush must have fallen over the room in those few seconds before Bishop Dan's reaction. "You're all ex-communicated," he blurted out in a tone of voice some saw as frustration, or perhaps anger at the man who'd stood up to him.

Dad and Grandpa were in that group. You can probably imagine the shock Mom and I felt when we heard the news as the men came to the lunch table.

Our life would never be the same again.

After some days or weeks when tempers had cooled, Bishop Dan offered re-instatement of membership to any men who would admit they had done wrong by standing up to the authority of the bishop and challenging the rules of the church.

Everyone except my father, grandfather, and Ike Smoker accepted the bishop's offer and admitted wrong-doing. These three men, in good conscience, were already moving on – to the Weavertown Amish Mennonite Church, where fast-growing businesses like Ike's were both accepted and supported.

I don't remember any complaining, or ranting and raving – or judgment – from Dad or Grandpa. Instead, I saw a sense of humor, which probably hid the humiliation they might have felt. Or maybe they just thought they had done what they had to do, and the ex-communication was simply the resulting price.

The men were shunned by the Amish Church community, along with their wives who followed them to the new church.[30] Still, they didn't complain – they just

---

[30] *Shunning,* also called *Meidung,* is defined by Dr. John Hostetler in *Amish Society* (1980) as "the practice of restricting member associations with persons who have been ex-communicated (or *banned*)." The Biblical instruction is that one neither "eat" with such a person or "keep company." (I Corinthians 5:11) "The Amish today practice Meidung as taught by their founder, Jacob Ammann," says

took it, and moved on, knowing they were no longer part of the Old-Order Amish community.

A few good Amish friends, like Aaron and Ruth Fisher, stayed in touch over the years, but our family life with them was never the same again. We lived in two different worlds.

Dr. Hostetler. "*Excommunication from the membership* is exercised after the offender has been properly warned and remains unwilling to desist from his transgression, divisive teaching, or rebellion." *Amish Society*, pp. 86-87.

17 | Daudy's Visit

The Saturday after Dad's ex-communication, I heard loud male voices in the kitchen that sounded familiar. So, I ran to the bottom of the stairway and listened through the crack in the back part of the door that was open just enough for me to figure out what was happening.

Daudy was yelling at Dad while Mom and Mommy quietly sat by the sewing machine in the far corner, pretending to work on a project.

"You have no idea what this will do to your children," Daudy yelled. "They won't belong anywhere."

He mentioned my name, arguing that I was too old to adjust to this change, and I wouldn't fit in anywhere else. "*Yes,*" I thought to myself as I watched all this from the crack in the door. "Daudy knows this won't be easy for me!"

Dad kept trying to explain his reasoning for standing up to the bishop, but Daudy wouldn't listen. His temper had flared up to something I was seeing for the first time. His shouts rang from the bottom of his voice, and it was obvious that he didn't like Dad's decision to move on.

There was no discussion that day about Ike Smoker's hay elevator factory, because Daudy didn't want to hear about it. He wasn't interested in Ike's revolutionary invention. His only concern was the division it would bring to our family. He knew Mom didn't want to leave the church – and he was right.

For a few months, Mom remained in the Amish church, still attending services until she could "think things through" in her own mind. Then she too left... but with a great deal of respect for her parents whom she always wanted to please. Mom wasn't a rebellious daughter by nature, though she did have a history of expressing her thoughts in a kind but firm way. Like the time she put tidbits of horse manure in Dad's chewing tobacco pouch. She *had* nicely warned him.

I didn't like hearing the two men argue that day and was afraid it might change our family relationships, but that never happened. The angry words between them didn't recur and life went on as usual. Except for a bit of shunning from Mommy and Daudy to my parents.

They weren't mean in the way they did it, but they did follow the basic rules of their church.

We continued to visit Daudy and Mommy at their house and they came to ours, which included a holiday meal the day after Christmas. But suddenly, I realized they were not supposed to eat at the same table with my parents. Neither were they permitted to accept anything my parents handed them, or to ride in a car with either of my parents behind the wheel. If my grandparents had been caught not doing this shunning, they might have been ex-communicated too – by their own bishop in the Buena Vista Church. Or, they might have gotten off with a warning.

Daudy may not have wanted to shun his daughter. Especially since his mid-western friends, like Henry Miller – the Amish bishop in Goshen – might have had a different view about such things. Shunning, when practiced among the Amish, was meant to inflict pain, so the wayward person would repent and return to the fold. Some Amish believe that such wayward souls who leave the church after baptism cannot go to heaven unless they confess their wrong-doing and re-join the community. Others simply see leaving as a choice. One can choose to be Amish, or not. They see salvation as a personal issue, between each person and God, which is a totally different way of looking at things. I don't know where my grandparents stood on these issues, since I never asked them – nor did they offer the information on their own. Mommy seemed apologetic, at times.

"I don't like this" (*Ech gleich des net*), Mommy would often tell my mother as she set things on the kitchen table for her daughter to pick up. She also apologized for the opening between the boards of the extension table when we were invited to a meal.

That crack was seen as a way to separate my parents from everyone else at the table, including their own children since my siblings and I sat on the end with Mommy and Daudy, which of course was hurtful. But Mom and Dad never complained. They understood it as a church rule and didn't seem to take it personally. That's the way I saw it back then, but it must have been humiliating for them. I regret not having asked them about it.

Mom's parents also always honored the shunning rule not to ride in a car with either of my parents behind the wheel, with one exception. Daudy once agreed to ride home with Mom – on a weekend – when he wasn't feeling well.[31]

Figure 21: Aunt Miriam, a family matriarch. Photo by Cathy Kornfield.

---

[31] Mommy had just passed away a few months before this incident and Aunt Miriam, who lived next door in the farmhouse, was planning a weekend trip. Aunt Miriam told Mom that Daudy didn't want to be alone, because he wasn't feeling well, so Mom drove to his house, inviting him to stay with her for a few days. He accepted the invitation and the ride in Mom's car. I dropped what I was doing that weekend, packed a bag and spent two days and overnights at my parents' house, knowing that Daudy was sick.

"Mommy's not here anymore and I'm tired," he told me. "I've lived a good life and I'm ready to go. I've been to every state in the U.S., except Hawaii and Alaska, and to parts of Mexico and Canada." A few months later, at age 82, Daudy died of a heart attack and was buried in the Amish graveyard at the crossroad of Mt. Vernon and Buena Vista Roads – alongside Mommy, four children, and Christian Petersheim (Aunt Miriam's husband who died in 1976, at age 56).

Aunt Miriam later moved into the *Daudy haus*, where she lived alongside her children and grandchildren until the end of her life, at age 94. The *Daudy haus* is now a beautiful vacation spot for people who want the farm experience in the "Buena Homestead," now owned by Aunt Miriam's son, Christian Petersheim, Jr., and his wife, Ruthie, who live in the main part of the farmhouse.

18 | EIGHTH AND NINTH GRADE

I was in the second half of the eighth grade when we left the Amish Church that spring. A new Junior High School had just been built at the edge of our town for seventh and eighth graders who were being bused in from the one-room secondary schools throughout Leacock Township. Amish kids still attended public schools since their own schools had not yet been established in our township.

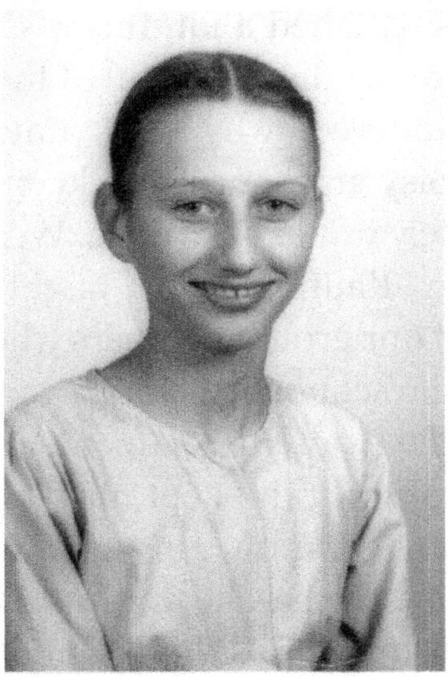

Figure 22: The author, 8th grade picture.

This new school was no fun for me. It was boring, compared to the previous three years in the one-room school next door, where Mr. Roy Denlinger had been our only teacher for grades five through seven. He had been transferred to the new school, but I didn't end up in his homeroom. So, I was missing his sense of humor, his interest in all the students, his emphasis on the arts... and most especially the extra recess time he gave us to play baseball on nice days.

I was crazy about baseball in those three years at Mr. Denlinger's school, and I especially liked hitting home runs. I blossomed as a student under his tutelage, even though I was never a teacher's pet like Levi Esh, the math whiz, or Barbie Smoker and her sister, Malinda, who got better grades than I ever did back then.

There are no words to fully describe the boredom I felt in my eighth-grade homeroom, except that I "acted out" with a lively group of students who sat in the left-hand corner of the room. Galen, Barbie, Lizzie, Rebecca and I exchanged notes, laughed a lot, threw spitballs from our desk, and were totally disrespectful of the teacher.

I often wondered why Mr. Kauffman did not discipline our noisy group or try to keep us quiet, as Mr. Denlinger definitely would have done. Were confrontations difficult for Mr. Kauffman, or might he have been protecting one of our group members whose parents were good friends of the school principal?

Oh yes, I must not forget to mention my English teacher, Mrs. Brabson, who kept me from total boredom that year. She taught grammar in a way that actually made sentence structure seem easy and important. But I was also fascinated by the stories she told about her handsome son, Bob, who was a student at Villanova Law School.

I wasn't the only star-struck girl who liked those stories and "gawked" at Bob on Fridays after school whenever he stopped by to pick up his mother. A few of us would stand by the front door until their car drove off to the City of Lancaster where his mother lived.[32]

Figure 23: Intercourse 200th Anniversary poster.

That summer, after our town celebrated its 200th anniversary, my school records were transferred to ninth grade at the Weavertown Mennonite School where learning became fun again. But that year triggered problems with Dad, when he didn't approve of high school and college for me, even though our new church community was in favor of it. That's a topic for another book.

[32] Years later, when Mrs. Brabson's son Bob and I dated for a while, I felt like I knew him. I had heard stories about him back in eighth grade, but of course, he had changed by then… and so had I.

19 | The Transition

The ex-communication of my father and grandfather will go down in my family history as an event to remember, like a bolt of lightning that suddenly hit us...

This ex-communication was perhaps most difficult for my mother. But Dad and Grandpa took it in stride. They rode the wave with a positive approach to the situation and quickly moved on to other things, which included a new church community.

My reaction as a fourteen-year-old girl was somewhat different. New people, places, and things replaced the old, leaving me with a kind of culture shock. Of course, I was excited about the convenience of the new car that showed up in our driveway and the electricity that transformed our house and barn, but my mood quickly changed when I lost my Amish friends at the end of the school year.

Losing those childhood friends was incredibly painful, since I didn't have a fully-developed adult brain to figure it all out. I wasn't told much either, but fortunately the transition took me to a new school where I made new friends. The pain eventually sparked my interest in psychology, sociology, and therapy – and a satisfying career, launched after a college degree. Ultimately, I went on to complete two additional degrees, while working full-time.

Over the years, I would marry two supportive men whom I loved, then lost to illness. Jim was a businessman from Mainline Philadelphia who passed away of a heart attack after eighteen years together, and Patrick was a Lancaster attorney who I lost to leukemia after thirteen.

It's never easy to recover from pain or opposition of any kind, but at age fourteen – and throughout life – I moved on to things I really wanted, sometimes against all odds, and always with support and a great deal of respect for the values of my Amish upbringing and the influence they had on me.

Of course, there were other influences in my life: people I haven't been able to mention in this book, the push and pull of my DNA, my spiritual leanings, the higher level of education that came my way after we left the church, and definitely my two husbands. Yet my Amish upbringing was already woven into the core of my being – its warp and weft as integral as the air I breathe.

My upbringing wasn't perfect, and nothing ever is, but it was unusual... never to be forgotten. This includes the mystery of my father and grandfather's excommunication that I'm only now beginning to solve in my own mind.

Figure 24: Abe and Priscilla Stoltzfus (the author's grandparents), 1954. Taken shortly after the ex-communication.

Figure 25: Gid and Lizzie Stoltzfus (the author's parents) in their later years.

20 | My Family Values

The stories in this book have helped me understand the family values (or ideals) of my Amish childhood, which influenced my parents and grandparents in the way they lived their lives, and raised their children. Of course, no one is perfect in the way we live out our values. We can only do our best.

Writing this book has given me a better understanding of my own values, which were influenced by my Amish upbringing and the example of my parents. Of course, I didn't totally buy in to all the family values, because of personal needs – like an education beyond junior high school. Quitting in the eighth grade was a cultural value, but I wanted more schooling. I liked learning new things. Plus, I wanted a professional career of some kind, which required a college degree and beyond.

Now, after studying my list of family values, I'm surprised to see my buy-in at a high level. Eleven values on that list somehow have become my own. Three did not.

The basic values of my Amish family:

Meaningful or satisfying work that pays the bills and makes people happy.

A strong work ethic, which includes the ability to focus on one's goals, a determination to reach those goals and the discipline to get things done.

Camaraderie, fun, and a sense of humor that softens the harshness of the work ethic.

Teamwork, where everyone does their best – as they work toward a common goal.

Self-employment – and flexible work schedules.

Strong family ties – including extended family like grandparents, cousins, aunts, and uncles – where people help each other in healthy ways and everyone does his/her part.

Strong community connections where people are there for each other, which includes the absence of judgment and gossip.

Partnerships in marriage, with well-defined roles where people understand their specific responsibilities in things like child care, work, finances, and authority.

A personal desire or need to help people in healthy ways where one doesn't feel used, or taken advantage of.

Careful spending, with money or investments set aside for future needs.

Gratitude to God for his many blessings.

A grateful, non-judgmental attitude that is quick to forgive one's self and others.

Working alongside children, as an example of what it means to be a good Amish person.

Making a good living on an eighth-grade education, followed by job training from a parent or employer who is good at what he/she does. Learning by example.

I'm not suggesting that every Amish family has values exactly like those I've listed. Amish families are all different, even though there are cultural commonalities.

The town where I grew up has changed drastically since I left in my early twenties, and so has the family farm.

Banks, coffee shops, and a few other businesses in the town are kept busy with local customers. But tourism seems to have taken over, especially in the summer months. The farm has been converted into Watson Run Housing Development, and a few other businesses, like "Stoltzfus Homestead" and the executive office of "Stoltzfus Meats," owned by Myron Stoltzfus, one of many cousins on my family tree.

It is also important to recognize things were changing for the Amish in the Intercourse Church District while I was moving on – getting my degrees in sociology, counseling, and education. The economic development of the post-war boom (and a fast-growing Amish population) drove up the price of Lancaster County farmland, to the point where not every able-bodied Amish couple could afford to buy a farm – required as the best way to raise children.

Family businesses were eventually seen as an alternative to farming in this church district. And a new bishop allowed it.

Amish people described this bishop as "a peace-maker who cared more about the needs of his people than the rules... although he cared about those, too." He saw the inevitable changes that had to be made and preached against the evils of industrialization that could destroy the "soul of the Amish culture" – what we outsiders know as values, traditions, and beliefs.

That new bishop was my grandfather's youngest brother, Stef.

ACKNOWLEDGMENTS

I'd like to thank Cathy Kornfield for standing by me while I wrote this book and for contributing in so many ways, including the photo on the cover. I'm also grateful to my mother for believing in me and the book I wanted to write about my family. Thanks to Sue and John for coming around to it, and to my father who would have liked the book if he were still with us.

A very special thanks to Demi Stevens, my editor and publisher, for her expertise, enthusiasm, and caring support in guiding me through this delicate process, and for her nudge to stop the writing and get on with the publication. Thanks to Chuck Sawicki for introducing me to Demi, to Herb Fisher's contribution from his photography collection, and to Joe Revelt for his valuable suggestions. Thanks also to my friend, Susie, and others, who encouraged me to take the risk in writing this book. Much love and appreciation to my late husband, D. Patrick Zimmerman, for making it financially possible for me to write, which led to this book.

Much gratitude for sharing memories of my family goes to Priscilla Herr, Reuben Stoltzfus, Randy Gamble, Barbie Esh Lapp, Anna Huyard Esh, Mel Lapp, Millie Stoltzfus, Mary Etta King, Jeanne Lapp, David Lapp,

Miriam Petersheim, Davy Stoltzfus, Ann Smucker, Ann Albright and others who wish not to be mentioned.

About the Author

Ann Stoltzfus Taylor, Ed.D., was born to a well-known Amish family in Lancaster County, Pennsylvania. Founder of Ann Taylor Publications LLC, and author of *Born Amish, The PEP Chart,* and *Step Into Your Brilliance,* Dr. Taylor is a graduate of Eastern Mennonite University and earned a doctoral degree from Temple University. A thirteen-year stint as a parole agent with the Pennsylvania Board of Probation & Parole, near the beginning of her career, expanded into a counseling practice as a career counselor and therapist, among other things, like management training seminars and teaching as an adjunct instructor at Lancaster Center of Penn State University.

Learn more at www.dranntaylor.com

Made in the USA
Monee, IL
12 March 2021

62568205R00090